THE
MINISTER'S EVERYDAY LIFE

THE MINISTER'S EVERYDAY LIFE

BY
LLOYD C. *assel* DOUGLAS

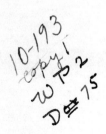

NEW YORK
CHARLES SCRIBNER'S SONS
1924

THIS BOOK IS DEDICATED
TO THE HONORED MEMORY OF A MINISTER:

ALEXANDER J. DOUGLAS

AN INTERPRETER OF LIBERAL THOUGHT AT A TIME
WHEN IT WAS NOT UNCOURAGEOUS TO BE PROGRESSIVE;
A COUNTRY PASTOR WHO CONSIDERED NO DAY TOO COLD,
NO MUD TOO DEEP, NO JOURNEY TOO LONG, IF HE MIGHT
EASE SOME BURDEN THROUGH THE PROFFER OF A
FRIENDSHIP THAT ASKED LITTLE AND GAVE MUCH

PREFACE

No vocation has created a more voluminous literature concerning itself than ours. Most of these books, written for and by preachers, relative to our profession, may be read with profit.

Even when the author's technic seems ill adapted to one's own disposition and mental habits, it always makes one want to preach better sermons after a session with a book treating of practical homiletics; and many a jaded minister has been galvanized into a higher potentiality by some sincere colleague's stirring summons to achieve more power in the pulpit.

His friendly counsel, too, concerning the solution of parish problems and the better performance of pastoral duties—perchance quite useless when considered as a method—invariably prods one to a surprising outlay of honest zeal to do these things more joyfully and industriously. We cannot have too many books of this sort, produced by active members of our profession.

It is to be observed, however, that a striking similarity of treatment distinguishes this type of literature. No matter how widely they may differ in temperament, training, and capacity, it seems that when ministers adventure upon fraternal admonition to their fellow craftsmen, they inevitably pursue the well-worn trail of their predecessors. The first mistake they register is their attempt to cover entirely too much ground in the course of a single volume. This blunder is, of course, only a sign of their excellent intent. They are so eager to help their brethren to a fuller and happier ministry, that they canvass the whole field of this vocation, unable to pause very long at any single phase of it.

The conventional beginning of such a book is phrased in hortatory terms. Here we are, they say, dedicated to the holy ministry. It behooves us to be sincere. Not much good can come of our pulpit performances if we are mere actors. Let us make sure of our recommitment to our task. As pastors, our profession is so heavily charged with responsibility that it almost frightens one to consider its demands. And because this is, in very truth, the first and greatest fact at issue, the author customarily addresses himself to this part of his book with such vigor and at such length that by the time he has done reconsecrating us to the job, he has used up about a third of the paper his publisher has assigned to him for the recording of his ideas.

This much achieved, and when our adviser is satisfied that we are sufficiently repentant over our laziness and properly ashamed of our poor workmanship, he talks to us about the science and art of preaching.

Advices on homiletics, whatever their source, are so uncannily alike that the recipient may be pardoned for suspecting the authors of collusion. Much time is spent with the fundamentals of voice culture, respiration, and whether the sermon should be delivered with or without notes or manuscript. If the writer himself happens to pursue the method of walking the floor, talking to himself, on Saturday nights, with the expectation of speaking as he is moved by the Holy Ghost, next morning, he is apt to talk about the sermon that is read from a manuscript as if it must be delivered in the manner of one reading the minutes of the last meeting. If he is a manuscript preacher, he is likely to refer to the extemporaneous method in terms which fail to elevate the adherents of that practice to upper seats in the synagogue where the intelligentsia are wont to foregather.

Two-thirds of the book now having been written, the typical author of counsel to ministers turns his attention to the duties of the pastoral office. By this time he is growing weary. He remembers what he has been told by others, and feels safe in repeating it. The minister should study all forenoon, and call all afternoon. He should visit the sick, console the sorrowing, and be on the alert for opportunities to be helpful to his fellow men. Not infrequently a daily programme is suggested, itemized by hours, which is about as useful as a crutch to a lame dog. What we need, apparently, is some technical literature, in our line, specializing on the details of the minister's pastoral life and the everyday demands of his office.

The medical profession offers an excellent example in this matter. When doctors write to doctors, they restrict themselves to some narrow field which they till intensively. One man produces four hundred pages on the eccentricities of the thyroid gland; another compiles nine dollars' worth of information on osteosarcoma; another limits himself to a discussion of the remedial agents used in the treatment of septic conditions. These men have nothing to say, in such works, concerning the honor, dignity, or ethical imperatives of their profession; not that these are negligible considerations, but because that phase of their calling deserves separate treatment.

A little while ago, in a brief series of essays, published in *The Christian Century*, I addressed myself to the younger members of our profession concerning some of the practical activities involved in our business. Judging from the voluminous correspondence which these articles produced, and the eager questions asked relative to other pastoral problems of equal importance to those under discussion, there is room for a book on this subject.

There will be a minimum of talk, in this volume, about the necessity of our being thoroughly consecrated to our task. It will be assumed that all this is fully understood and appreciated. There will be next to nothing said here about our pulpit ministry; although it will be quite impossible to avoid all mention of sermon-composition, seeing this is a week-day task.

It will suit my mood to speak by the process of direct address, mostly. I am offering my remarks to the youth of our profession—seminary students in training for the ministry, and young preachers who are meeting many of their pastoral experiences for the first time. I shall assume that the reader knows very little about the practical solution of parish problems. All the venerable veterans in the service are therefore notified that the observations about to be vouchsafed are intended for the inexperienced youngsters of our profession. Our elders and betters will find very little here previously unknown to them; and it is cheerfully conceded that this thesis might easily be elaborated, to its vast improvement, by scores of them, in phrases more felicitous and in a tone of higher authority.

Having staked off my claim, I invite the novices of our vocation to drape themselves about the old man's knee, and turn an attentive ear. If the oldsters wish to stand by and observe the clinic, they may consider themselves welcome. The seat of the scornful, however, has been temporarily removed from the operating pit to make room for the class.

Advance notice is hereby posted that I do not propose to be hurried. Neither shall I feel under compulsion to lay out all of my remarks after the manner of a new real-estate allotment. This is not a class in engineering. If it pleases me to ramble from the motion before the house, at any time—lest I forget to mention some matter that bobs up, inadvertently—I shall do it without so much as a by-your-leave. I may thus face my task with greater freedom; and, anyway, it is an old man's right.

Certain phases of the articles published in *The Christian Century*, to which reference has been made, are reproduced here, with the consent of the editor, to whom I acknowledge indebtedness for this favor.

CONTENTS

CONTENTS

THE
MINISTER'S EVERYDAY LIFE

CHAPTER I

THE MINISTRY AS A PROFESSION

TO take immediate advantage of the privileges of senescence, let me speak of my own feeling toward the ministry as a profession.

I have recently celebrated the twentieth anniversary of my ordination into the Christian ministry. I entered this profession, which was also my father's, with both eyes open to most of its exactions, many of its sacrifices, and some of its rewards. Now that a score of years have been spent in it, were I again to choose a vocation, knowing all that I do to-day about its requirements and recompenses, I should unhesitatingly ratify my earlier decision.

I am not seeking to convey the impression that these twenty years have brought no problems. Many a sunset has found me disinclined to sit down at the piano and sing "A Perfect Day." There have been hours when, if somebody had offered me a nice, fat part as a shovel-wielder in a ditch, with the understanding that my immediate burdens would be lifted, I should have been disposed to follow him. To the best of my knowledge, this is the common lot of all

men, regardless of the nature of their employment. They may expect an occasional dull day when life is something quite other than one grand sweet song.

But, by comparison and contrast, I am convinced that our profession is about as free of annoyances as any useful vocation. Casual observation will assure you that all of the professions, and every other sort of retail business involving personal, hand-to-hand contacts with the public, confront problems equally or more difficult to solve. Perhaps a certain amount of obstreperousness on the part of a small percentage of one's clientèle only makes the job more interesting. At least, much aid and comfort may be had through that philosophy when things are going at sixes and sevens in one's work.

Traditionally it is believed that the preacher suffers more than other men from the petty irritations of his office—annoyances put upon him by persons who, either in zealous ignorance or excessive overvaluation of their own administrative and advisory talents, burden his life until even the storied grasshopper of Ecclesiastes has naught on him in that respect.

If it is not positively immoral to seek solace by contrasting one's portion with that of one's less fortunate neighbors, the preacher may comfort himself by observing that his lot is no harder than many another whose actual re-

wards are not so abundant as his own. How, for example, would you like to be the "trouble clerk" at the telephone exchange? Perhaps it would be a good thing for some of us if we might contrive to swap jobs with these people for a week. We might return to our ministry in a more contented state of mind—assuming we still had our minds. What manner of poise must be exacted of him who, all day long, listens to the whines and snarls addressed by the infuriated to the "adjuster" whom the gas company has appointed as its official goat! What must be the length, breadth, and depth of her tranquillity who conducts the "complaint bureau" in the big department store! One marvels at her spiritual resources—or is she paralyzed on that side, so that she doesn't feel the blows any more? What kind of patience must the ticket agent possess who, every day, must listen, respectfully, to queries conceived in ignorance and brought forth in stupidity! How must the workman suffer who dares not, for the sake of his children's bread and butter, offer any back talk to an insolent and unjust foreman!

But these people, you say, are hardly to be compared to us. Their station in life is different. Very well; if that is the trouble, consider the case of the most prosperous merchant of your acquaintance; owner of his business, we will say. This man is obliged to deal, diplo-

matically as possible, with all manner of troubles from without and within his establishment. The problem of petty pilfering alone demands the services of an expensive staff of experts in detection in the larger shops. These employees are not policemen, with clubs and badges and raucous voices. They are there to handle, as graciously and considerately as may be, the surprising delinquency of persons from whom much better things than larceny might have been expected. They are there to make theft look as innocuous as possible to the astounded husband who comes in, upon polite request, to pay for something that accidentally fell off the counter into the lady's hand-bag.

Moreover, the merchant is obliged to deal, tactfully as he can, with the case of those who, while they do not actually steal from him—fearing to be apprehended—perform the equivalent of it by taking his goods out on approval for a brief period, but long enough for them to break faith with him, and violate his confidence in them. The party gown is worn, that night, and returned to the store, next day, refused. The gloves are rendered unmarketable, but not unreturnable. Everybody has seen dull people handling dainty gift cards and de luxe editions, with dirty hands or grimy gloves, while the merchant stands by, helplessly, watching his good property depreciate to serve no better cause than to safeguard the sensitive feelings of

ostensible customers who have learned a very great deal more about their privileges than their responsibilities.

The merchant, then, deals with the thief, the near-thief, the liar, and the fool every day! Not once in six months—every day! He has added to this the problem of laziness, incompetency, disloyalty, and dishonesty among his employees. The most trusted man he has may turn up with a shortage. His best buyer may prove to be a grafter. The oldest clerk in the place may be operating a "fence" for crooks. He never expects to solve his problems. He only wants to keep them under fair control. For, while he is dealing, on the one hand, with a small percentage of thieves and half-wits, both in his patronage and his employ, the larger number, by far, are normal; and these he counts upon to provide him with his business prosperity.

The captain of industry, in the grip of economic conditions which, however he may deplore them, are problems he must accept, mostly as they stand, carries burdens not very well understood by the rank and file of the people. On one side, he deals with an increasingly large number of workmen to whom the amount in the Saturday pay envelope is of much more concern than the quality of the labor they perform or the volume of production. Back of them, and prodding them to acts of insubordination, are the professional trouble-makers whose positions depend upon their activity in the cause of industrial discontent. It is difficult for the big man in industry to ascertain exactly who is loyal and who is not. He may be disposed to deal generously with the loyal and efficient. Frequently he is disappointed and chagrined to find his trust violated. On the other hand, he is the servant of a directorate. Back of the directors are the stockholders. Both sides—the capitalistic forces and the laboring element—are out to get all they can, almost by any hook or crook. Add now to this his problems of competition with similar concerns whose management may be utterly unscrupulous—and you have dished up a mess that is far from palatable.

Consider the physician's problems. Patients who quit him for another doctor never bother to explain their action. He does not know whether he unwittingly said something that caused offense, or was found unsuitable professionally. He is frequently called out at 3 A. M. to deal with the hysteria of somebody who needs only to be spanked; but he is expected to be gracious, attentive, and anxiously concerned. He may be doing his utmost at the critical stage of a pneumonia case, and return, after an hour's absence, to find that upon the advice of Auntie McFudgeon, next door, his treatment has been abandoned for hers. He may be on the way toward success with some tedious convalescent demanding rigorous hygienic and dietary regulations, and learn, one day, that his patient has discarded the whole regimen to espouse Christian Science. The chances are that after he has spent many weary weeks toiling over a ten-year-old whose legs were shrivelled with infantile paralysis, and has just begun to notice the first faint signs of improvement, he discovers that the parents have decided to avail themselves of the services of some flashily advertised chiropractor who, six months earlier, was operating a jitney bus. He has been nursing a crippled back, with tireless devotion, and, maybe, no hope of material reward beyond the consciousness of good service rendered, and find, some day, that the patient's silly parents have permitted an alleged divine healer to remove the brace, to the complete undoing of all his labor. Yet one does not hear him complain; because, while he is dealing with a certain element that lacks the judgment to co-operate with him to their own advantage, there are many more who can be depended upon to obey his orders and treat his counsel with respect.

How would you like to be the superintendent of the public schools, and spend a generous portion of each afternoon listening to fond mothers of impeccable small boys as they narrate the injustices their offspring have suffered at the hands of the gargoyles who pretend to teach, and irate ignoramuses who come to quarrel over the brand of biology taught in the high school?

So, if you will calmly survey the trying problems of other lines of business than ours, you may reach the conclusion that our profession is about as free as any of them from the most disgusting irritations and annoyances.

Sometimes I like to think of myself as an employee and the church as my employer. Considering our relation to be that, I am only fair and honest when I say that, as an employer, the church has treated me squarely. Frequently I hear of ministers whose experiences are not so pleasant, and I have no occasion to doubt their word. Sometimes it happens that a sleepy congregation will permit itself to be controlled by a small lay leadership whose judgment is poor. Out of a situation like that there may arise a great deal of bother for the minister. It is possible for a very self-conscious official board to make things hard for their spiritual adviser. Sometimes the prudential committee is disgustingly frugal; made so, however, by long struggle to stretch an insignificant total of receipts over an alarming bill of expenses. And if it seems imperative that the minister must be cautioned about preaching on this-that-or-the-other subject which infuriates our wealthiest contributor, let the preacher bear the fact in mind, however indignant he may be, that the fiscal problems of the church are very real to the men who have become custodians of them. Thirty pieces of silver loomed up rather impressively to the man of Kerioth, after he had been squeezing mites and farthings for three years in an effort to preserve the solvency of the Apostolic College. Don't misunderstand me. I am not trying to apply the soft pedal to any pulpit utterance which needs to be made in the cause of pure and undefiled religion. When a thing simply has to be said, it has to be said, even if the whole Board of Trustees walks out in a body, and the wealthy contributor has a fit! But, sometimes it is something that really could go very well without saying. At all events, do not forget that the prudential committee has its troubles. I am informed that it is at this point that many ministers experience their chief annoyance.

My memory goes back to some of the trying events in the ministry of my father. Entering the profession after fifty, and by way of circumstances which, while they constitute the most interesting story I know, were not conducive to the receipt of calls to city churches, his pastorates were rural charges. He never aspired to any other fields than these. His salaries were small, which did not matter greatly, for his own wants were simple, and my mother was an excellent manager. I never once heard him complain about the size of his income. An unfailing sense of humor sustained him, sometimes, in moments when, but for his ability to recall some petty performance on the part of his official boards as a screaming farce, he might have been completely overwhelmed with disgust. Having left an honorable and lucrative law practice to become minister to a group of struggling little churches, at a salary of four hundred dollars per annum, plus a house, it is doubtful if he could have endured the slow grind of voluntary poverty with any other attitude than the ability to see its humorous aspects.

Uncle Noah S., superintendent of the Bethel Sunday-school, when approached by a member of the Bethel church, shortly before Christmas, soliciting a contribution toward a gift for the minister, replied that inasmuch as he had been their Sunday-school superintendent for twenty years (which was all of fifteen years too long for any man to be in that position), he thought it would be pleasant if the gift were made to him instead of the preacher. Said Noah: "Make me the present, and I shall give the minister the equivalent of it." And because he was the most important man in the congregation, subscribing twenty dollars a year to the church, and superintendent, and Deacon for Life, they complied with his request, hurrying to the parsonage, however, to report the incident.

Having already discovered the exact dimensions of Uncle Noah's microscopic soul, my father waited, with eager curiosity, the promised dénouement. Holidays were long passed, and it had begun to seem as if Noah had forgotten, when, one Sunday, our family was invited to drive home with the old fellow for dinner. After the feast had been properly disposed of, and his populous household had been called into the big living-room where the guests waited, impatiently, the bestowal of an equivalent of the gold watch he had received from the Bethel Christmas-tree, Uncle Noah strode majestically into the foreground, his hands behind him, evidently holding the gift. He made a little address, in which he expressed his loyalty, admiration, and friendship for his pastor; expected to make him a present; couldn't think of anything he valued more highly than the product of his own pet bees, which he had come to love as tenderly as a father loves his children; and, with a flourish, brought forth a quart jar of strained honey!

My father replied, gravely and graciously, with words which I would give much to be able to recite *verbatim*. As nearly as I can recall, he told Uncle Noah that while the gift was far too precious to use in any ordinary manner, due to its sentimental value, it would henceforth occupy an honored place upon the mantel at the parsonage; and it would be our delight, pursued my father, to tell the beautiful story to all the friends from Bethel who, from time to time, sat with us about our grate. I don't know what the watch was worth, but I am very sure my father, through the years that passed thereafter, had a great deal more fun with that jar of honey than he ever could have had with the watch.

In another parish it was customary for the "joint council"—representatives of all the official boards of the six churches in that "charge" —to assemble at the parsonage on a certain Saturday afternoon at the close of the church year, to settle up. There was a deacon at the Mount Hope church (I have changed the name of that institution because a few of Philip's heirs and assigns still reside in the neighborhood, and I bear them no grudge) who, for many years, had hauled the last load of clover-hay to the preacher as a gift. On the occasion of the annual meeting of the "joint council" to which I refer, the Mount Hope congregation was found to be four dollars and seventy-five cents short of meeting its not excessive pledge toward my father's salary. Philip was probably worth fifty thousand dollars, and there were three or four other farmers in that church who rated as highly in this world's goods. The deputation from Mount Hope tugged at their whiskers, at a complete loss to solve the problem of their deficit. Presently a light broke in the eyes of Philip. "Parson," he said shyly, "I reckon I'll hev t' charge yuh fer that air clover-hay, this time." My father smiled and replied: "Very well, Philip; how much was it worth?" "About five dollars, I cal'late," Philip answered. "Then I owe you a quarter, don't I?" Philip chuckled and "'lowed" that was so. Father handed Philip the coin, and Philip put it into his pocket. There were eighteen men present, and not one voice was raised in protest. These men loved my father in their dumb, stupid, cloddish way, and he knew it. Doubtless, they all wished this transaction might have eventuated in some other manner; but they had no remedy to offer.

Of course a situation like that is the preacher's own fault. I do not presume to pass censure upon my father. If he blundered, it was an error of his tremendously big heart. He permitted people to impose upon him in this way. But, practically considered, I do not believe it was very good for their souls to be allowed to conduct themselves so. It would have been in the interest of their salvation to have heard a few remarks, occasionally, on the fine virtue of being decent to their minister as an employee.

In my own experience, there has been no meanness shown toward me by the officers of

the churches I have served. I trust it may
not sound too bumptiously impertinent when I
say that I would not have permitted it, in any
case; but it never became necessary for me to
clamor for my rights. As to my wages, I have
always been paid, promptly, all that was due
me. My income, through the years, has compared very favorably with that of the majority
of those who subscribed toward it. Moreover,
I am disposed to believe that it always came
pretty close to being my earning capacity, for
if I had been worth very much more I would
have had bids for my services in larger amounts.

In these days when so very much is being
said about "an underpaid ministry," I often
wonder if we have not talked more than necessary on that subject. It has never been my
right or duty to inquire how many of my con-
fessedly underpaid colleagues might have increased their wages by donning some other
uniform, but I have some private opinions on
that matter locked in my desk to be published
posthumously when I am safe from the remarks which verily would be their reward.

If one may take the risk of being irritatingly
candid, the less talking you do about "an underpaid ministry" the brighter will be your
own chances to refute that statement as it
might apply to your case. Most people are
too much occupied with their own affairs to
make a meticulous invoice of their neighbors'

actual value. They accept others at their own self-rating, just as the fire-insurance agent takes your word for it that you have a thousand dollars' worth of furniture in your house. Only when there has been a fire does he come around with a pencil and tablet to investigate the exact state of your worldly effects. Likewise, it is only when your personal value to society is in question that the public goes to the bother of making a serious inventory of you. Ordinarily, it rates you at your own appraisal of yourself. If, therefore, you go about saying to a generation that estimates one's worth mostly in terms of money that you are underpaid, most people will catalogue you with all the other underpaid persons of their acquaintance—an estimate which will not only do you no credit but actually jeopardize your chances to improve upon your condition.

It is one thing for a man voluntarily to assume a life-work inadequately remunerated, preferring to derive his happiness from his opportunities to serve than from pleasures purchasable with a large income. It is quite another thing when, having entered upon that profession, open-eyed and fully informed as to its financial limitations, he sourly frets and complains. Doubtless, if I were speaking to laymen, I would add another paragraph or two, relative to this matter; but I am not now talking to them, but to you. If your people are

behaving meanly toward you in this matter, refusing to give you as much as you are rightfully
entitled to, you would better leave them; for it
is a clear case that you are doing them a bad
turn by remaining to be treated in a manner
that militates against their own sense of honor.
Resign, and let some other man come in and
do for them something that you have apparently been unable to do. Accept the call to
that other church which has offered you the
larger salary representing your present earning capacity. Very brutally—if no other church
has indicated that you possess a higher earning
capacity than you now have—what makes you
think you are getting less than you are worth?
Let me repeat: if I were speaking to laymen,
I might approach this subject from another
angle.

You will find, if you have not already discovered it, that there are many subtle temptations
in our profession. If some ministers are full
of whine and whimper about their hard lot,
their exacting duties, the heavy burdens put
upon their time and strength, it is largely the
fault of a well-meaning laity. One of the popular delusions about our business is that it
overworks us. Of course this is a pet American
obsession. Seven persons out of every nine, in
this country, are indulging in such foolish talk
about themselves, obviously to create the impression that their services are in great de-

mand. You will do well to avoid contracting this silly habit of chattering about how busy you are. Beware of beginning it; for it is as dangerous as a drug addiction. Once you get your little piece down pat, and find yourself repeating it, on all occasions—too busy to eat, too busy to sleep, too busy to study, too busy to do much but talk about how busy you are— you'll never get over it! It becomes an obsession, a mania, a psychoneurosis! If you've begun it, stop it, while it is yet day!

Well-meaning old ladies in the congregation will tell you that you are working yourself to death. If they prefer to believe this, so be it unto them; let them believe it. But do not permit them to make you believe it. You are not working yourself to death. Not often does a minister step into an untimely grave from overexertion. It is a known fact that persons of our profession are considered a preferred risk by life-insurance companies. One splendid old insurance company restricts its clientèle to ministers, and is thus enabled to offer rates which not only insure you at a much lower cost than you can buy such protection from any other concern, but, at the same time, insures you against life-insurance agents—which is not to be sneezed at by one who places so high a value upon his precious time.

Of course, if it should come to the sorry pass that you do actually work yourself to death, which is extremely unlikely, that will not be an unbecoming way for one to die who has pledged himself to follow the leadership of a man whose career closed at age thirty-three—but the chances of your surviving the exactions of your job are excellent, if the records in the office of the Board of Ministerial Relief mean anything at all.

When, therefore, solicitous friends seem disposed to mourn your impending departure, a tragedy superinduced by heavy labor, embrace the opportunity to set them right on this subject. It will give you a chance to offer some constructive counsel concerning the importance of our disposing of this i..sidious "busy bee" which has fatally stung the poise of so many otherwise efficient people. Many members of our profession are making themselves utterly ridiculous with their running about, watch in hand, mopping a perspiring brow, as they attend, apparently single-handedly, to the world's salvation. Perhaps the greatest contribution you can make to this hysterical generation that gallops through life as if pursued by the Furies is in offering a living example of poise and tranquillity. He whom we attempt to serve once said: "Come unto me, all ye that labor and are heavy-laden, and I will give you rest." This was one of the most intriguing of His invitations to the public to adopt His way of life. It is to be doubted if you and I, as His ambassadors, will ever be able to make this alluring precept sound sincere and convincing unless we cultivate other habits of mind and conduct than those which now propel us about, panting and puffing, in a state of perpetual stampede, as we rush from one mighty event to another. I hear them saying at big conventions: "The King's business requireth haste!"   Well, maybe so; but try to plan your own daily programme so that you will remind people more of a prophet than a medal-winner of all the track events at a field meet.

I have discoursed upon this matter at some length because it well deserves some serious thought. You young fellows are beginning your ministry at a time when the whole world is bewildered, distracted, mentally dishevelled! If you give it anything worth having, that bequest will be a new sense of calm and quiet trust; a sense of steadiness. You cannot do that if you live your own life on the run.   Moreover, there is a whole heap of near-humbuggery involved in the things we say, or imply, about our overcrowded schedule. The majority of us have sinned egregiously at this, from the least unto the greatest.   Not long ago, a really great man of our profession, having finished an epoch-making speech, upon being pressed to remain for a moment to meet a committee where his counsel might have been helpful, announced, breathlessly, that he had just time to make his train; had to get that train to make connections with another appointment. He went to the hotel, and spent the remainder of the evening as the centre of a group of admiring friends, who had persuaded him to stay over until morning. I heard the story told, next day, in a company where there were a half-dozen young preachers present. They chuckled. They will forget the incident, in time, I dare say. "Clay feet?"—they will admit it of their idol; but they will remember that his head was gold. Now that good and great man was not conscious of perpetrating a wilful deception. I can imagine that he has come by this state of mind a little at a time. He began it by answering all comers, when they inquired: "Well, doctor, how are you to-day?" "Oh, I'm busy, desperately busy—driven—driven—driven!" Pish! Tush! And nonsense!

People will be hovering about you with hot-water bottles, urging you not to go out minus your overshoes; sending you ear-tabs, wristlets, shawls, and cushions at holidays. They will be dreadfully stirred up if you have a cold in your head. Your sneeze will excite more anxious comment than your neighbor's gall-stones. Should you pound your thumb with the hammer, the casualty will be town talk for days. The poor dear hit his thumb—he did. They can't help it, apparently. That's the way every church treats every preacher, so far as I know.

You'll have to make up your mind to bear it with whatever grace you have. Once in a while it gets to be about all a regular he-man can stand; but there is positively no way to deal with it, for it is all done with the very best intent in the world. They honestly love you, partly for yourself, but mostly for the office you hold. We Protestants may chatter as glibly as we like about "a universal priesthood of all believers," but race memory, wherein is built the layman's reverence for his spiritual father, still drags the public back to the old idea. You are in a peculiar line of business, and don't you forget it! The last thing you want to be, on earth, is a priest, perhaps; but that's precisely what you are, in the opinion of most people, albeit they might stoutly resent your being called by that title. You are, whether you like the idea or not, more of a symbol than an executive. People who want to do something for the Lord, and are unable to express themselves adequately in that direction, are going to take it out on you! They will pity you. They will pity you because you have to work so hard. If you are caught in a rainstorm you will surely be wetter, in a given length of time, according to their judgment, than any other kind of a man. Your discomfort will be more acute. You will be more likely to suffer from your experience. I say, make up your mind to go through it. It is our common lot who belong to the priesthood. But, listen—don't get to thinking this way about it *yourself!* In the name of all that's honest, don't pity *yourself!* If they want to crowd their affectionate little attentions upon you, for the reasons indicated above, let them. It's good for them. In many cases it is about the only tangible expression they are able to make of their love for the church. But you must be steady in your own mind! Don't let it spoil you! Many ministers, of bright promise in youth, of unquestionable talent and exceptional gifts, have permitted themselves to be utterly ruined by the devotion, solicitude, and well-meant attentions of their people. If you cannot be a real man in this business, get out of it while there is still time to take up some other profession! We've quite enough mollycoddles in our guild now without bidding for any more. If this sort of thing is spoiling you, look for another kind of a job. The ministry isn't the only career in which a man may acceptably serve his Master. Sometimes I think that for some men it is probably the only career in which they can't!

When Jesus wants to go up to Jerusalem, and it is evident that the trip will involve grave danger to His life, the senior deacon pleads with Him not to do it. Mary breaks a box of ointment and pours it over Him. The disciples are distressed because, having wrestled

unavailingly with a storm, they must awaken
Him to ask counsel. All this because they
loved Him. They loved Him as a friend; they
loved Him more as a symbol of the eternal.
But it did not spoil Him; and although He
had been the object of the warmest tenderness
they knew how to exhibit, and the most sentimental solicitude it was in their power to express, when the hour came for Him to push
them all away, that He might rise to the full
stature of His courageous manhood, the records
show that the martial spirit with which He
shouldered His last burden compares very favorably with any other act of heroism ever presented to a world in which deeds of valor have
not been few.

As a little lad, I was aware of the fact that
our place was always waiting for us, when we
arrived in a new community. If it is not
stretching a point to speak of our "social position," in the small towns wherein our lot was
cast, that position was assured from the moment we stepped off the train into the arms
of the reception committee—bless 'em!—nice,
comfortably stout matrons who would insist
upon kissing one, just because one was the
minister's laddie. To be sure, we were poor,
and our clothing was probably not of the prevailing vogue; though I don't recall that this
fact ever gave me any concern as a little boy.
People could not dress modishly on four or five

or six hundred dollars a year—not even in the days when the great American dollar was a more notable institution, as to its purchasing power, than now. Our furniture was about what you would imagine furniture to be that had been purchased out of that kind of an income, and taken on rough rides, again and again; for rural preachers did not remain very long in a "charge" in those days. But, our place was always made for us, socially. My father was one of the most influential men in the community. He did not have to earn it, though he could have done so. It was his by right of his office. My mother was looked up to by the best women of the town. She should have been; she deserved to be—but she came by her position as my father had come by his: it was the office that made us.

Whatever we did was more or less a public event. Never having known any other mode of living than this, I have not permitted it to cause me much worry. But, even so, the lot of "the preacher's kid" is not always an unmixed delight. The same sort of fawning solicitude which is the minister's portion, by virtue of his position, is exhibited, to a degree, toward the whole household of the prophet. If the youngster has any sense at all of the serious obligation he owes his father, to walk circumspectly, he is almost sure to develop into what the parish calls "a model boy," which will make him magnificently despised by his contemporaries. Presently he will face the problem whether he is to be, in very truth, the fine little fellow who will add lustre to his father's reputation as a prophet, in which position he will live the life of an outcast in his relationship to his natural social group; or decide to show his schoolmates that he is a regular feller, despite his hereditary place in life.

Now, if you never were a "preacher's kid," and haven't had a chance, consequently, to experience the sensations involved in that position, keep these things carefully in mind when you deal with your own boy's problems. Remember that while your boy is the minister's son, he is a boy. If he is approximately normal (I say "approximately" advisedly; for it is scarcely possible that he can be entirely normal for reasons just indicated), he is almost sure to make mistakes of disobedience, wilfulness, and the general cussedness to which our human flesh is prone. Sometimes he will seem to be a bit more naughty than absolutely necessary, even for a normal boy. This will be due to his anxiety to show his friends that there is nothing uncannily holy about him, merely because he dwells under your roof. Be very sympathetic. Believe me, his problems are grave—far more grave at age fourteen than yours were at twenty-one! Let him live a normal life, in so far as that is possible. So soon as you are able to do so, send him away to school. You had better send him elsewhere to an academy than to the high school in your own town, if you can possibly contrive to meet the expense. Violent protest will be raised, I am sure, against this declaration. It is possible that you, yourself, are shouting: "No! No!" So we disagree on that point; do we not? That doesn't necessarily make either one of us right. As for myself, when young, my love for my father was sufficient to hold me in leash against my natural inclinations to have some friends; but you may take my word for it that I was a very, very lonely little boy. And whenever I was felicitated, by our parishioners, for refusing to do whatever it was that the boys of my age were doing, against their parents' wishes, I despised them with all the fervor of a soul that was raging at the inhibitions put upon me by virtue of my obligation to my father. Deal with your boy very carefully and understandingly, or you take the chance of seeing him ruined for life. I mean that! It's just that serious!

Before you decide, however, not to have any children, on account of the risks involved in attempting to bring them up properly, you should be informed that, not infrequently, a minister's child turns out well, in spite of these conditions. In "Who's Who," one name out of twelve is of a minister's child.

Now that I have indicated a few of the perils of a profession that makes one an influential citizen and an object of public attention, I should have stated only the negligible end of the case were its advantages to be overlooked. It surely means a great deal to a man to occupy a place where he can capitalize every talent he possesses. When the young physician comes to town, he may, by dint of diligent application to business, make a place for himself in the course of five years. For a long time he must content himself with dignified starvation, and be satisfied with a practice that would make him laugh if it were not quite so pitiful. If in five years he has arrived, townspeople comment pleasantly upon the startling suddenness of his general acceptance in public regard. Let him remove to another town, no matter now capable he may be, and he has it all to go through again. The same thing goes for the lawyer. But the preacher is a person of consequence before he has had time to unload his freight. This is a perquisite of our office which, while it has its perils, has also great advantages. Such a singular privilege carries with it a large responsibility. Not only may the minister step immediately into a place of prominence in the town where his work is located, but he must accept that distinction and make adequate use of it. Let him bottle himself up, and refuse to avail himself of the honors extended to him, by virtue of his office, and he diminishes his usefulness to that community in exact proportion to the depth of his seclusion. Keep carefully in mind the everlasting fact that every privilege which one may honorably accept, in all professions and in all human relationships, is attended by a commensurate responsibility. Do not permit the exceptional privileges of your profession to spoil you, or lead you to a fatuous overvaluation of yourself, for they are not extended to you because you are William Henry Smith, but because you are an ambassador of God.

CHAPTER II

THE PASTORAL RELATIONSHIP

WHETHER a minister is to succeed or fail in a given pastorate depends considerably upon the manner in which he begins his work in that community. Ours is a profession in which personality counts for a great deal. If, in the process of establishing connections with your new parish, the conditions are favorable for you to express, pleasingly and effectively, your personality, the chances are good that your ministry in that place will be successful. If the conditions are unfavorable, you may find it an up-hill road, all the way.

In your first parish you will, of course, be indicted at once on the charge of being young. Our business requires, for its proper performance, a certain amount of self-possession and self-confidence. You will not have much of that, for obvious reasons. This is, we will say, your first work. You are just out of the seminary. In an effort to counteract the almost inevitable smile on the faces of the saints as they behold your attempt to perform, with an air of long accustom, certain services which they have good reason to believe is your initial experience of the same, you may be almost ghastly in your seriousness. A far better attitude for you to take, in this predicament, is to begin your ministry in your first church with the candid declaration that you have it all to learn—which will not be much of an exaggeration. Assure them that they must stand by, patiently ready to make suggestions, offer counsel, and see to it that your blunders are reduced to a minimum. In this way you can impute to your congregation the responsibility for training you to be a minister to them and the other churches you are to serve in the future. A naïve attitude of simple-hearted confidence in their willingness and ability to steer you rightly will commend you to their interest and affection much more surely and quickly than any pitiful attempt to dissuade them, by your assured manner, of their knowledge that you are a novice.

But don't carry this childlike ingenuousness too far. "Let no man despise thy youth." Some things about your profession will have to be learned by the unpleasant process of trial and error; some things you will have to ask questions about; but there are a few things you will be entirely confident of—matters in which your own common sense will offer advice —and, when you know you are right, go ahead! Don't spend the first five years of your professional life permitting multitudinous advisers, however well-meaning, to drag you about from one administrative policy to another.

Let us talk frankly about a few of these problems you are going to meet.   In the first place, you will be obliged to have it out with your predecessor.   No; he will not be there in person, but he will be there—never fear about that!   Either he will have been a dismal failure or a huge success, by the time you arrive. As a matter of fact, he may have been an ordinary, honest, capable fellow, whose ministry, while he was actually engaged in it, had excited neither cataclysmic applause nor hoots of disapproval; but by the time you are located he will either have been canonized or anathematized as a success or failure.   They will tell you all about him.   If he is remembered in affection, you will become almost too well acquainted with his story for your own comfort.   His particular points of merit will be recited until you know them by rote.   If that is the sort of thing they like, you may decide, they undoubtedly like that sort of thing—so you will be tempted to imitate, in so far as you are able, the strengths of this good man.   He was a wonderful mixer, an adept story-teller, the life of the party. Perhaps your own temperament does not qualify you to shine, with a brilliant lustre, in that rôle. If that is the case, don't make a monkey of yourself in an effort to be the exact replica of your predecessor.   You, too, have some admirable points of strength, though they may not lie in the field of comedy.   Ascertain early as possible what features of your ministry are most effective; what things you do best, and with the finest results; what things are most rewarding to your own sense of duty fulfilled —and concentrate on those things. If they are vastly different from the specialties of your predecessor, so much the better. You will insure against comparisons and contrasts in which one of you may come out badly.

If your predecessor was a failure, you will hear about that, too; and unless you have more magnitude of mind than everybody else in this sinful world, the reports of this poor fellow's blunders will cause you but little pain. By the artful sparring of some undisciplined demon in your subconsciousness, over whom you have no control, it may come to pass that you involuntarily manœuvre conversations with the faithful to a stage where it is possible for them to chant another dirge over the remains. Of course you will come back with some pious palliation of his mistakes, which will but send the layman to his guns, again, to take another crack at the brother. I never cared greatly for David's requiem over Saul. He had been the old gentleman's gadfly for many, many years. Yes; I am well aware that Saul's attitude toward David had been reprehensible, but David always managed to take care of himself. Whether he meant to do it or not, he undermined the king's influence, won the affection of

the people, made himself a member of the royal
family, and let Saul in for a wretched administration. I have always felt that David should
have delegated the job of composing the requial
poem to somebody else—Abner, for example.
For the inevitable effect of David's singing affectionate sentiments relative to his late sover-
eign, in which he imputed to the old chap certain virtues he did not possess, only made the
royal minstrel more solid with his constituency.
The less you say about your unsuccessful predecessor, either in rebuke or commendation, the
better for you. Keep away from the subject!
If you observe that the conversation is beginning to skate around on the thin ice adjacent
to that hole, divert its attention to something
ten thousand leagues away!

What kind of a person are you going to be,
in your attitude toward the people? There
has been quite a clamor, in recent years, for
what is known as a "human" preacher, by
which the public means that it prefers a minister who is full of jovial kindness, ready wit,
and an unreserved spirit of comradeship; a
man who can be talked to without restraint.
And because the young preacher knows that
this is the case, he is sometimes tempted to be
just a bit more chummy and confidential with
certain of his pet parishioners than is necessary
to qualify him as "one good sport."

Now and then a youthful prophet needs to

be warned against an attempted insulation of himself against congenial contacts with the members of his parish; but not many men, entering our profession to-day, are in jeopardy of paying the penalty of cloistral habits or monastic mood. If any caution is in order, it must be a plea for more quiet reserve. He is very fortunate to whom has been vouchsafed the gift of wit and a keen appreciation of humor; but when this fact becomes the chief attribute predicated of him by his friends, the more serious and important functions of his ministry are rendered difficult.

I take no pride in the fact that I am a solemn old owl. Doubtless it were better for me if I knew more funny stories, and was more of a cut-up. Sometimes I have almost envied a popular colleague of whom the neighbors said: "Oh, our new minister, Reverend O. B. Merry, came to call on us the other night, and he certainly is a brick! Laugh? We all just howled!" But there is a temptation for the witty preacher to become slightly stampeded by the maudlin appreciation bestowed upon him; and, unless he enjoins a fine restraint upon this indulgence of his delightful gift, he may live to recall, with humiliating self-abasement, the occasions when he had played the buffoon and clown. There is a happy middle ground somewhere between depressing solemnity and riotous foolishness which the minister will do well to locate, for his

own safety. He must not be a frigid killjoy;
but in his endeavor to avoid the gown and cowl
it is not necessary for him to put on cap and
bells.

Here, again, I am obliged to remind you that,
whether you relish the idea or not, you are, in
a sense, a priest. As a young minister, you
must keep this fact in mind. The public will
seem to want you to be exactly like the layman. People want to see the preacher with
his coat off and his sleeves rolled up. And just
because they do want to see him with his coat
off, there must be some very excellent reason
for his keeping it on until the occasion arrives
when there is a much better reason for his
taking it off. Everybody seems to have a
strong desire to get back of the stage to see
how the storm and lightning effects are produced; but once he has done so, the inquisitive
is never again quite so deeply moved by these
phenomena.

Now, there is a curious psychology at work,
here, in your relations to your congregation and
the general public. You are the exponent of
that which is holy. You, yourself, are a norm
of conduct in your community. Don't shy off
at that, as a responsibility you are unwilling or
unable to assume; for it is a fact, and the sooner
you accustom yourself to the idea the better off
you will be. The people must have standards
for all their action. You are a standard in the

field of conduct. They all wish they might be better, morally, than they are; but most of them are not going to the bother of improving themselves. You are their moral norm. They are eager to decrease the length of the gap between their morality and yours. They may not care to attempt that action from their end of the line; so they are relying—some of them —upon your decreasing this distance from your end of the line. They wish they were like you. They are more likely to try to make you come to them, and be like them, than to go to you, and be like you. I hope I am making myself clear. That is why they want you to take off your coat, and be "human." That is why they chuckle so joyously over your slang. And if, when you slice a drive on the golf course, you should, on a certain great day in that town, let out a vigorous expletive sounding suspiciously like "dammit!" their appreciation will know no bounds! They are rapidly bridging the moral chasm between themselves and you, and it seems to make them glad. You are a "human" preacher. Yes, yes; but your ministry to them is breaking down, and both you and they know it! Think these things through carefully; for it is difficult to amend whatever relationship you establish with people in respect to these matters.

The young minister dares harbor no silly notions to the effect that he must assume a "thus-far-and-no-farther" attitude toward his lay friends; but he should be aware that the less his parishioners know about his choice of breakfast cereals, the weight of his underwear, the name of his favorite hair tonic, his aches and pains, the little habits and whimsies of his private life, etc., the more effectively he will serve them in the graver emergencies of their lives when they look instinctively to him for spiritual guidance with an expectation probably far in excess of his actual ability to exercise the same.

It is better, therefore, not to talk too much about yourself, your little likes and dislikes, your plans and hopes, or your former exploits, in college and elsewhere—regardless of their character, whether they are to be pointed to with pride or viewed with alarm. Your reminiscence of the boyish prank you and three other fellows played upon old Professor Darius Powder may evolve into a felony which, had justice been served, would have jailed you for life, ere your tale has passed into the revised version. I hope I do the saints no injustice. For the most part, they are the best people on earth. But, you see, they like you so well that everything you say is of interest. They try to repeat your best yarns about yourself to the neighbors. The neighbors, equally interested, perhaps, endeavor to spread these tidings as far as they will reach. By and by, somebody, whose affection for you is under somewhat better control, takes up a mangled fragment of your minstrelsy, and yelps it so discordantly that you, when you hear its echo, will call down imprecations upon your own head for being so foolish as to load your enemy's gun, and wait his leisure to pull the trigger.

It is extremely hazardous, also, to talk about your wife and children. The quaint remark that little Bobby made to his small sister Geraldine, in the course of a juvenile theological debate, may be delightfully funny when you tell it; but the chances are too many that by the time this merry quip has been passed through its sixth translation, it will have assumed certain heretical tendencies which may reflect badly upon the type of religious instruction offered under the minister's roof. And your wife's decision that it is cheaper, in the long run, to buy canned peaches than to can them herself may be a moral issue of great heat and four dimensions by the time the narrative has been manhandled for a month. Let me repeat: nobody wishes to do you or yours a wilful injury. They are interested in all your goings out and your comings in, from this time forth and forevermore; your downsittings and your uprisings. You are at once their employee, their priest, their moral mentor, their pet, their property. If you think you are not up to the strain of it, go into some other line of business, for you cannot alter these conditions.

Be very prudent about extending confidences to intimate friends in the parish, concerning administrative matters, and under no circumstances whatever may you talk to outsiders about any problem at issue in your church. You must not tell anybody of your disappointment over the fact that the Board of Deacons had not seen fit to approve your request for a more expensive contralto. You may consider it entirely safe to explain to the musical Stafford family, who put you up to this scheme, why it failed to be executed, but it is not safe to do so. The Staffords are very nice people. They would cut off a hand rather than do you damage; but they are human. I do not want to imply that you are to discredit the ability of any one in your parish to keep a secret; but it is so very much wiser not to have secrets. You will sleep better o' nights if this is your fixed policy, and it will positively insure you against some of the most awkward situations that can possibly arise in the pastoral relationship. Incidentally, you might permit your wife to share your sentiments on this subject, if they meet with her approval. The minister's wife who, in sheer loyalty to her husband, makes her disappointments articulate when the prophet has been unsuccessful in executing some pet plan of church administration, has unwittingly dealt him a wallop from which he will be long in recovering. The chronicles of our profession are loaded with the sad tales of brilliant and industrious ministers who, because their wives were exceptionally gifted in the high art of private conversation, talked these fine fellows into the shades of Never-never Land. You will find it to your advantage, also, to avoid talking too freely about parish matters in the presence of Robert and Geraldine. They are but little children, and you cannot expect them to exhibit, by tactful silence, a more excellent judgment than you yourself display when you give them the custody of information which should be restricted to your professional activities.

Don't talk too much about the details of your business. Don't confide to Brown how you contrived to win the friendship of Smith; how you encouraged a larger subscription to the church from Jones; how you retrieved the waning interest of Robinson. Doubtless you showed good strategy in all these movements, but you certainly were not much of a statesman when you let Brown handle the machinery whose operation should be a secret known only to yourself. What leads you to think that Brown may not consider it so clever a thing that, in genuine loyalty to you, he will report it to a friend, in testimony of your effectiveness as a minister?

Never tell anybody anything that was said to you in the course of a conversation wherein a confidence was extended. Understand me—

I do not mean that you might be so imprudent and unethical as to violate a confidence. I mean that if, in the course of your conversation with White, which he opened by telling you that he thought of selling his car because his wife was leaving to spend the winter with her parents—a conversation which he developed into a confession that he and Mary hadn't been hitting it off very well, lately, and heartily wished there might be some better solution for their problem than a separation—should you be so injudicious as to remark, next day, to Black, who is in the market for a car, that you heard White say he wished to dispose of his car—and Black goes to White and inquires— and White asks Black where he heard that the car was for sale—he may have some reason to wonder how much more you told Black, in confidence, concerning your mutual friend.

Increasingly, people will be inviting you to share their personal problems. Parents will confide to you their difficulties with their half-grown children; wives will tell you their troubles with their husbands; husbands will—not nearly so often—tell you their troubles with their wives; girls and boys will tell you about the difficulties they are having with their parents; men will come to confess their struggles with the things that have all but done them in— mostly drink and gambling; persons of both sexes will intrust you with the secrets of their love-affairs. Indeed, if there is anything in the whole range of private information that may not be disclosed to the minister, I should be greatly interested to learn what it is. This phase of your ministry belongs exclusively to your professional life, and must not, on any account, get mixed up with your domestic life. These things are not confided to you in your capacity as a private individual, who has a wife, and children, and intimate friends, but solely in your capacity as a priest. I do not mean that you are to refuse to divulge these things to your wife for fear she might tell them. I mean that you are not to tell her because she has no right to know, herself! As a private individual, even *you* have no right to this information.

Somebody remarks: "Oh, isn't it just awful! —Mr. Witherspoon is going blind—and the doctors say he will be entirely sightless inside of the next three months!" You are not to say: "Yes, it is very sad. I knew it was coming, last January." Or, some one says: "Oh, have you heard that poor Mrs. Martin has a cancer?" You are not to reply: "Yes, I knew about that, six months ago!" Your wife announces surprisedly: "I was told, this afternoon, that the Greenes are getting a divorce." You are not to say languidly: "Ah—so they're getting it, are they? I knew they had it in mind." Keep your professional life and your home life distinct, in respect to all confidences. In the long run, this policy will provide its own reward.

I still have certain misgivings lest I may be misunderstood by your wife, in case she should read this book. I am sure she is a person to be trusted with a secret; but there are some things she has no right to know. Moreover, when she has been made custodian of certain secrets, it often places her in very embarrassing situations. I am fortunate in being able to offer this advice without the slightest feeling of restraint, inasmuch as not one misunderstanding or embarrassment has ever arisen, in my own experience, due to an imprudent word from the lips of the lady who shares my fortunes.

By reason of the fact that you are engaged in a line of business which deals with life in its most holy and intimate relationships, be careful about safeguarding the seriousness of these matters. Cute little babies sometimes do amusing things on the occasion of their baptism. If other people want to tell the story, and consider it jestingly, that is their right, but not yours. Because it is not a long step from the sublime to the ridiculous, there will be occasional experiences, at very serious moments, in your ministry, which would beguile a grin on the face of the gloomiest ascetic who ever practises self-flagellation. Plenty of people can be depended upon to tell the story with high glee. They cannot be blamed. The less talking you do about it, and the less attention you pay to it, the better. Nothing that ever happened at a funeral, for example, is funny. Whether you are a fundamentalist or not, you may put this down as a fundamental. This is a hard-and-fast, seven-days-of-the-week, time-lock, sunk-hinge, twenty-two-carat fact!—there is nothing humorous about a funeral! You may be able, one of these days, to recall a few circumstances when it did seem as if matters were afoot, on such sad occasions, calculated to provoke a smile. You will have heard stories of unforeseen and awkward events which transpired, in the course of funeral services, experienced by other ministers. But you must never repeat any story—real or fictitious—anywhere, to anybody, concerning anything that ever happened at a funeral provocative of a smile; for the very excellent reason that you have no way of knowing that you will not be back, within a week, in that very house where your funeral yarn made such a tremendous hit, attempting to offer comfort to a bereaved family who cannot avoid remembering that you once found it possible to see something funny in a funeral. All such jokes are absolutely on the index, in our profession. It is unethical to tell them. If you want to relieve your feelings by relating your deliriously funny experience to your colleague, with whom you sustain an intimate friendship, that is a matter for your own good judgment to pass upon. Prudence suggests that even this would be taking a risk.

There is a certain school of humor which depends rather heavily upon diluted profanity to render it effective. You will do well to avoid repeating any story which requires the use of profane phrases. I am sure I do not know what there is about "hell" that seems so funny. If there is a hell, and if the allegations predicated of it are correct, it is to be suspected that nothing very funny ever occurs in that institution. If there is a "devil," and his traditional disposition has been adequately set forth, he lacks something of being jovial. But, many a yarn would fail to classify as a humorous narrative were it not for some episodal reference to the place of everlasting torment or the person whose sole occupation is in the market of misery. Anybody can tell a story with swear-words in it and draw a chuckle. You should provide yourself with a repertoire of stories which do not depend for their success upon the number or intensity of the cuss-words involved.

There are a host of undeniably witty stories based upon quaint perversions of Bible texts; but you tell them at the risk of making it difficult to repeat these passages of scripture correctly in the pulpit without stirring the mem-

ory of certain people present who cannot help
adverting to the good story you once told in
this connection. The tale of the little boy in
Sunday-school who offered as his scriptural contribution, "Many are cold, but few are frozen,"
had best be told by some one other than yourself if you expect, some day, to avail yourself
of one of the most significant statements in
the New Testament.

Shortly before leading you into the belief
that I am hoping your conversation may be
literally restricted to "Yea, yea," and "Nay,
nay," let me speak briefly of a profitable type
of communication which involves no risks whatsoever. You are to be loaded to the gunwales
with stories about people you have known whose
experiences are worth passing along to others.
You should be in possession of a wealth of narratives for the sick-room, concerning the fine
type of Christian sportsmanship displayed by
people under heavy fire. As your experience
increases, you will be able to recall the case of
the man whose physician had given him only
ninety days to live, and who sent for you, not
to condole with him, but to tell him how he
might most effectively invest his last three
months in high-grade service to his fellow men.
You can tactfully tell the story, to the chronic
neurasthenic, about the woman you knew who
spent her last eleven years in bed, hopelessly
crippled with rheumatism, practically dead ex-

cept for her beautiful mind and radiant soul; and how men and women, singly and in groups, used to visit her for the sole purpose of sitting for a little while in the presence of one who wore her chains with majesty.

The admonition you might heartily wish to extend to your friend and parishioner, the manager of the wheelbarrow factory, concerning the "human element in industry" can easily avoid any appearance of impertinence if projected through a narrative. Having called at the office of Mr. Scroggins, the wheelbarrow man, and having queried him about the success of his recent fishing trip, you can be reminded of a fishing expedition you once made on the Au Sable River, near Grayling. You will tell him all about the trout-hatchery, up there, and of the interesting Hanson family who originally planned and financed the undertaking for the benefit of sportsmen. This will set you going on the subject of "Old Man" Hanson, who owns practically all the lumber industries in his town, and for forty years has kept so close to his men that he sustains a first-name acquaintance with them; how Mrs. Hanson continues to go about with baskets of jellies and other goodies, visiting invalids and shut-ins belonging to the families of their employees; how there is a little heart-to-heart conference, every morning at nine, in which all the foremen connected with the shops are asked for suggestions and advice relative to the proper conduct of the Hanson business. You can tell him there never was a strike in Grayling, and never will be, so long as the "Hanson brand of Christianity" is working on full time. Tell the story, sometimes, of the man who said to you, after having told you of a long-term sorrow in his life, which he could neither amend nor relinquish: "I've made up my mind, parson, that it's part of my job!"

Plan your conversation so that when you leave a place, where you have visited, the people will know but little more about you and yours than they knew before, but are possessed of certain new ideas about themselves: their possibilities, their responsibilities.

The better preacher you are, the more gifted you are sure to be in respect to creative imagination. A sermon is a creation. Good sermons may not be produced by unimaginative preachers. No mental department of yours will be given more constant exercise than your imagination. This talent is at once a gracious gift and a perpetual peril. You will fall into the habit of speaking hyperbolically and metaphorically. Certain dull people, under the impression that the minister should always speak "by the card," will take you literally when you had hoped to be understood as speaking allegorically. Pare down your superlatives. Deal vigorously with your exaggerations. Don't let anybody form the impression that you are careless in respect to the truth. A blunder at this point may heavily discount everything you say, in the opinion of some one who has been given reason to doubt your veracity, even though he should have come by that opinion in so small a matter as your description of the bass you caught, last summer, or the number of strokes in which you holed out at the Country Club.

One of these days—apropos of the pastoral relation—you are going to leave Pikeville. You will have been there four years, we will say, and everything has gone along very nicely; but your church in Pikeville has always known that you were due for better things, if going to a larger town, a more prosperous church, and a more comfortable salary is a better thing. Assuming your denomination to be one in which congregations extend "calls," the process is likely to proceed somewhat as follows: Some Sunday, perhaps three men—strangers in town —will appear in your congregation. They will not sit together. But they will come and go together. They will ask the clerk at the hotel what he knows about you; and he will not know anything, good, bad, or indifferent. He may not even be able to inform them as to the location of your church in that little town. They arrived late on Saturday night, and will leave Sunday night, or early Monday morning. They are busy men, and must be back home as soon as possible. The only persons they will be able to consult, concerning you, will be people who may know nothing of local church affairs. The visiting committee will hear you preach. Chances are you will have been "tipped off" by some friend that you are to be looked in upon by a scouting party. If so, you will have two good sermons that day. Your people will notice the strangers in the audience. They will suspect the errand of these strangers.

If you have made a favorable impression upon the committee, you will hear from them. You will not hear from them in a week. They have several other eligibles on the string. Meanwhile, you have made up your mind that if the call comes from Blinkton, you intend to accept it. You begin to grow restless. You begin to think of your ministry in terms of Blinkton. You were there once at a conference. Pikeville shrivels daily into a place of decreasing significance. And then—one glad day—the letter comes, inviting you to preach a trial sermon at Blinkton. I'm not saying you should refuse to go and do it. Perhaps that is the only way you can make connections with Blinkton, and maybe you really should remove from Pikeville to Blinkton. I am only going to say that when and if you go to Blinkton, to preach a trial sermon, you appear there as one who has something to sell. If you stand pat on a fine resolution not to go to Blinkton to preach a trial sermon—informing that church that if it wants to hear you preach, the same can be accomplished by sending official representatives to Pikeville for that purpose—then, if Blinkton's interest in you is deep and sincere, and your conditions are met, and you are visited by a group officially empowered to do business—you are not a seller but a buyer; and you may take it from one who has served in both of these capacities that the latter rôle is much more satisfactory than the former.

But, however these negotiations may be effected, any keen anxiety exhibited by yourself to make early connections with Blinkton will militate against the success of your ministry when you have arrived there. The psychology of the salesman is far different from that of the customer. There is nothing reprehensible about being a customer. No business can be done anywhere, unless somebody is the customer. But, make up your mind which you are going to be in this case, and conduct yourself with the dignity befitting the rôle you have chosen.

You cannot expect to keep this matter a secret, very long, in Pikeville. Plenty of little tragedies occur in this connection. Possibly Blinkton gives you every reason to believe, through the private correspondence of your new friends in that place who speak emphatically, albeit unofficially, of the impending call, that you are as good as moved. I knew one case in which the minister, having been assured that he was going to receive a call, went home and resigned, preached a farewell sermon, filled his front yard full of boxes—and had to take it all back! He "got away with it" too; and remained where he was for a long term of years enjoying a successful ministry. But I doubt if any such performance is to be recommended.

Pikeville is going to know all about it. There are plenty of crisscross lines of contact between Pikeville and Blinkton, no matter how far apart they may be in terms of railroad-track. The thing for you to do is to be entirely honest, candid, and fair to everybody at both ends of the line, including yourself. You should tell your church officials—not outsiders; remember that!—of the movement on foot. Inform them that Blinkton has your case under advisement; that you have not bidden for it (if you haven't); that you do not know that anything is to come of it; but that you want to be the first to tell them, preferring that they should get the information from you, as their employee, rather than from some other source. No matter how it comes out, then, you will have preserved your own dignity and have kept the faith with them. They will honor you for your frankness and fair dealing. If the call from Blinkton fails to arrive, they will not put that fact down against you. There are plenty of churches in this coun-

try which are never going to give you a call,
as both you and the deacons know; and nothing more serious has happened than that Blinkton has been discovered to be one of them.
For a week after the blow falls, you will feel
depressed; but, cheer up. Hurl yourself into
the Pikeville job with fresh zeal. Nobody is
ashamed of you because some other church
turned your way—and then decided you were
not suitable.

If you are sufficiently poised, the way to
avoid a great deal of this sort of heartbreak is
to delay going mentally to Blinkton until you
have the call in your pocket.

Let us suppose that the call comes through
and you are now en route to Blinkton, at the
request of the officers of that church, to talk
over matters of business detail. They will be
very gracious and you will be a fine fellow.
You will be so fine a fellow, indeed, that you
may set yourself a pace that will make you
perspire considerably when you return, later,
to open up shop. Take your wife along on this
trip. She may not wish to go. She has not
been "called" to Blinkton, she says, and very
truthfully. But you take her along. Your
earliest contacts with the chief members of the
church in Blinkton, who are to be your closest
friends, supporters, and advisers, will be more
satisfactory if you form them with your wife
present. You are aware that you are a different

person when you are away without her—no better, no worse, but different. Make yourself known to these people exactly as you are going to be known by them in the future.

The trustees will discuss the salary. When you met them before, they were in your hands, and they told you they were paying Brother Brown eighteen hundred dollars, and the use of the parsonage. You were not informed that this was what you were to get, if you came, but you assumed such to be the case. To-day, you are in their jurisdiction. They will have a hard-luck story that would fetch tears to the eyes of an alligator. Business conditions are bad; the church has gone into the hole; there is quite a bit of floating indebtedness. Undoubtedly, within the space of a year, they can give you a raise; but, considering the fact that Brother Brown was an experienced man, who had been with them for eight years—and began at twelve hundred, and no house—and considering, also, the fact that you are but a young man, perhaps you could see your way clear to start on about fifteen hundred. Now you have met a serious predicament. The people of Pikeville know that you and your wife have gone to Blinkton to look at things. You have already fallen in love with Blinkton because you are regarding it as your future home. The chances are good that you will consent to be taken at a bargain; but, if you do, you make a serious mistake.

The only way in which most people estimate values is in dollars and cents. If you accept a call to Brown's pulpit for a nickel less than Brown received, you are confessing that you're not the man Brown was and you know it. Everybody will know it. All Blinkton will be informed of it. You came at a bargain. Perhaps, in time, you may grow up, and be as good as Brown was; but, for the present, you are passing through your novitiate.

Now, you had that experience to go through, doubtless, when you went to Pikeville, and accepted it as the most natural thing in the world. You were a novice, and admitted it. If they wanted to be small enough to beat you down when you were a mere fledgling, all well and good. But Blinkton's case is different. You are entirely justified in telling the trustees that if you are not the man Brown was, they had better shop around until they find somebody about his size. Have no fear that you are going to mess things up for yourself. If Blinkton really wants you, it will come through and do the right thing. Incidentally, you will win the silent admiration of every business man on that board. Even those who have been most ardent in their attempts to beat you down will admit to themselves that you are likely to succeed, if this is your way of doing business. Don't begin, in a new town, under the handicap of being known as something the committee grabbed off a bargain-counter. If they only had the wisdom to understand the psychology of this situation, they would know that it was to their own serious disadvantage that you should be started off, in their parish, with the story hanging to you that you had been bought cheaply—an inferior article.

Close up your affairs in Pikeville so that every time your name is mentioned in that town it will demand respect. Keep your work going at full speed, until the last minute. Perhaps several months are to elapse before you actually sever your connections there. Don't let things slump! Pursue your programme with diligence. Whatever plans you have already instituted should be executed with unabated industry and interest. But don't start anything new! Don't celebrate your departure by organizing some new society in the church—"The Heirs of Promise"—or something like that, to become a nuisance to your successor. Give him a chance for his life. Don't begin to patronize Pikeville, because only two trains stop there daily, whereas Blinkton has one-man street-cars, 'n' everything. These people have done a great deal for you, and you must not forget it. You went there as green as grass, and if now you are to be promoted, part of the reason for your advancement lies in the fact that they helped you develop. It is true that an excellent preacher can "make" a church; it is no less true that an excellent church can "make" a preacher. Leave them feeling cordially disposed toward you. Don't go with a hip, hip, hooray!

Meantime, during the period of your call and your departure, Pikeville will be looking around for a new prophet. Of course you will wish to be as sympathetic with that movement as possible; but the very best traditions of our profession certify that the less you have to do with that matter the better for all parties concerned. If you think you know exactly the right man, suggest his name. But don't get to meddling in the negotiations. This is their business and his. You will do him no service by giving him a glowing account of his pending opportunity. Let him make his way in, without too much assistance on your part. Always there will be some who can remember that you exercised yourself so diligently in your friend's behalf that they had to take him. This will be bad for him, whether he succeeds or fails. Don't be fond uncle to your successor. Let him hoe his own row. That's positively imperative to his making proper connections with the job.

You are now packing to move to Blinkton. You will now discover how rich you are in this world's goods. Perhaps it is at the close of the season—July, we will say. You are going to take a month's vacation before you begin at

Blinkton. The parsonage is being "done over," and it will be inconvenient for you to put your stuff into it now. You are advised to send your things to storage in Pikeville, and have the storage people forward them to you, later. Listen to me: don't you make any such arrangement. The storage man at Pikeville will sting you. No; I don't care a nickel's worth who he is. He may be the senior deacon. You gather up your traps and start them toward Blinkton. I wouldn't trust the typical moving-and-storage concern any farther than I can throw this house in which I am sitting.

Put your little things in small boxes. The smaller all your boxes are, the better you will like your possessions when they arrive. Don't begin your packing by putting the screw-driver and the hatchet in the bottom of the first box. Skillets and china make a bad combination. Wrap every piece of furniture in burlap. Burlap is much cheaper than furniture. Stay on the job and personally supervise this operation. When you pack your sermons, go through them critically, and select ten of the best ones. Take the rest of them down to the furnace and burn them; that is, if you really want to develop into a preacher.

Clean out the parsonage at Pikeville with a broom. Go over it again with a mop. Finish the job by polishing everything with a silk handkerchief. Some people may be able—have been able, I know—to leave an empty house a mess; but you must not. If there is a broken window-pane in the cellar, mend it. If your movers have skinned the paint off the front steps, repaint them. And thus you are off toward Blinkton with a clear conscience, and the people of Pikeville will rise up and call you blessed.

CHAPTER III

RECEIPTS AND DISBURSEMENTS

YOU have entered a line of business in which, if you perform it effectively, you can never become wealthy. You may marry money, or some rich relative may bequeath to you a legacy, or you may accidentally stumble upon some hidden treasure; but you must not expect to arrive at opulence by way of your profession. It simply isn't there; and whatever estate you contrive to amass will be more a matter of saving than earning.

The economic considerations of the minister's life are worth talking about; so we will give them some attention at this time. First, let us think about your receipts. Item one, of this exhibit, is your salary. Generally speaking, the more the church pays you, in salary, the more the congregation and the public will respect you, and the larger will be your opportunity to succeed as a leader in your community. If they are paying you starvation wages, it is because they do not think very highly of your ability. Without putting intolerable burdens upon them, you should insist that they provide you with an income not only sufficient to cover your necessities, but to insure you a comfortable margin for insurance and savings against the day of your non-employment. They have no right to have you in their employ on any other terms; and when you consent to serve them on a basis which permits them to be unjust to you and your family, you are only certifying that as a moral leader you are not a success.

This salary of yours should be paid promptly. The smaller it is, the more often you should get it. The church that pays a salary of fifteen hundred dollars a year, doled out in unstandardized lumps as it happens to be collected, sometimes as much as a month in arrears, should be forced to mend its business methods, or put up the shutters. Neither should this salary be extended in the nature of a gift. This part of the church's dealing with you is strictly business, to be negotiated in the same mood in which the factory pays its employees.

It has not been so long since the smaller churches supplemented the income of their pastor with donations. The custom may still prevail in some quarters, for all I know. Psychologically considered, the idea was not very good. It had a tendency to make the minister feel like a pauper, and placed him in a relationship to his congregation which was extremely awkward, to say the least. He was obliged to appear grateful for gifts which, quite frequently, were of no use to him; and accept, with an air of pleased surprise, a great deal of stuff which should have been marketed at the prevailing rate, and the price thereof appended to his salary.

When my father received a call to a new "charge," the promised reward was generally phrased: "Six hundred dollars in salary, the free use of the parsonage, and donations." Shall I ever forget those donation parties? There would be, perhaps, as many as six churches in this combination under the pastoral care. Each congregation would name a day for the descent upon the parsonage, loaded with munitions. Of course not every member of the congregation would appear in person. Some of them would send their gifts with the neighbors. But enough of the faithful would arrive to tax the housing capacity of our modest manse. Many of these gifts were of substantial value. Farmers used to come in with hams, sausage, apples, flour, corn, oats, and everything conceivable in the way of preserved fruits. The company usually arrived about 10 A. M., and stayed all day. The women brought huge baskets of provisions for the dinner. I am not saying that the social aspects of the affair lacked value; for it gave the people a chance to become better acquainted with their minister. Neither am I pooh-poohing the generosity thus expressed. But, when they were all gone, our house was due for a complete cleaning, from cellar to garret. Perhaps as many as a score of more or less unsupervised little children would have had the run of the place all day. The farmers couldn't help it if mud was fetched into the house on their feet. So, after the last cordial farewell had been spoken, and the ravens had flown away, and Elijah was left to reckon his accretions, the problem of making a fresh start in life was very trying. There was jelly on the banisters, mud in the parlor, chicken-bones in the best chair.

The first important act was to itemize our gifts with a view to ascertaining how rapidly certain things would have to be eaten if we proposed to conserve them before they spoiled. If the donation party occurred shortly after "butchering," in the fall, we would find ourselves almost embarrassed with our wealth in pork products. My resourceful mother always contrived to smoke and cure these meats so that there was but little, if any, loss; but it was a rather heavy responsibility to take proper care of so much stuff, on short notice. There was an unwritten law that the preacher could not sell any of these things; neither could he distribute them to the poor, unless he was willing to take the risk of seeming to think lightly of somebody's gift. Whatever the season had produced, on the farm, in greatest abundance, was naturally most in evidence at the donation party. Once there was an unprecedented crop of apples in the country. Our establishment was nearly suffocated with apples and every imaginable apple product. When the good angels had left, my mother reported that there were eighteen gallons of apple butter. On the verge of tears, she said to my father: "What in the world are we going to do with all this apple butter?" To which he replied cheerfully: "We'll paint the barn!" Of course I can't expect you to realize how deliriously funny all this was in our household. To understand it you would have to know my father's story, and what a curious experience it was for a man who had been a successful and well-paid lawyer to have come into a position wherein apple butter was offered in consideration of professional services.

This donation business, then, came along at frequent intervals. Six churches had it to go through; as did we. Six complete house-cleanings per year. Six trying experiences of figuring a way through and out of a wide assortment of more or less perishable provisions which could neither be sold nor given away. The farmer, of that period, never slaughtered cattle, and only rarely a sheep. He killed hogs. He brought nice bits of his hogs to us. It would have been absurd for us to buy beef when it was with the utmost industry that we could eat the pork donated to us. I have not yet entirely recovered an appetite for pork.

I do not recall that we were ever presented with clothing. We children were proud little rascals, and I doubt if we could have gone through that without a rebellion. We were entirely willing to wear the home-made garments fabricated by our mother's patient and inventive fingers; but I doubt if we would have consented to wear anything that had been previously on duty elsewhere. There are tales of ministers' wives who were presented with hats, capes, dresses, and shoes which had done service before they became her property. I cannot think that the Lord ever required anybody to suffer an experience like that.

Donation parties always afforded the members of the church an opportunity to know each other better. The women would appraise the various articles as they were brought into the kitchen, and many an interesting conference would result when some well-to-do family's generosity was called in question. "Him!—Peter Marks!—five pounds of salt and a peck of potatoes! He ought to be put out of the church!" There were plenty of times when they cheerfully bore one another's burdens; but on donation day they invoiced one another's burdens, at the parsonage, with undisguised candor.

Now I trust I am not making a mockery of the affection and loyalty of these excellent people when I smile over these events recalled from the days of my childhood. My father loved these genuinely good farmers, as they loved him; but if they had only known the depth of his self-abasement, as he consented to accept his living on such terms, they might have devised a different programme of recompense for him.

A little while ago, before I drifted into this reminiscent mood anent donations, I was saying that your salary is the first item in your list of receipts. Comes now the parsonage. While you live in that house, you are the custodian of it, and it is up to you to keep it in repair. I do not mean that the expense of all repairs should be borne by yourself; but, rather, that you should keep your Board of Trustees informed concerning its condition. Don't let this property run down. I am aware that there is a "Buildings and Grounds" Committee; but it is part of your job to see that church property does not go to rack and ruin. Fresh from a board meeting where much talk was had of the necessity for economy—one of the most popular topics of conversation at such conventions—you may be reluctant to report, to the proper authorities, that the cellar wall under the parsonage needs attention; that the front steps are ready to fall down; that the plumbing is out of kelter; that the electric wiring is unsafe; that the furnace is impotent. But, whatever may be the apparent desire for frugality, manifest by the Board of Trustees, you will get but little applause from these men for neglecting to inform them, promptly, concerning the need of repairs at your house.

While we are on this general subject, you may as well make up your mind to it that you are now, and are always going to be—no matter how conspicuously you may be located later —the actual custodian of church property; and if you think to win the approbation of your constituency by permitting their buildings and equipment to fall into decay, for the sake of paring down expenses, you are making a great mistake.   True, you are not employed as the caretaker of the church property; but you had better take care of it, nevertheless.   The congregation will forgive you an occasional slump in the pulpit but it will view with much regret and distaste an unmowed front lawn, an untidy back yard, an untrimmed hedge, a gate off its hinges, unraked leaves, broken fence-pickets, unshovelled snow and ice on the walks, and an old shirt protruding through a broken window of the attic, at the residence of the parson.

While you are ambling through your homily on Sunday night, some of your parishioners, whose upturned gaze indicates a state of holy contemplation of your sidereal remarks, may not be indulging in pious reflections at all. They are looking at an electrolier in the ceiling in which four lamps are burned out—the same four lamps which were missing last Sunday night and the Sunday night before that. Indeed, they are the same four dead lamps which were deceased six months ago. It is not your fault, of course. You are not the janitor. But, to be on the safe side, go over the whole plant occasionally, to make sure that such little matters receive attention. After all's said it is your responsibility and you must not ignore it. It will be a responsibility that you cannot shake off even in the years to come, when experience, industry, and talent may have won for you a position in which you have much more to work with in the way of property.

Much as you may wish it otherwise, the fact that the linen collars on the choir vestments are dirty is your fault. It is your fault if the church clock is ten minutes slow. It is your fault if, because the heating-plant has gone out of business, your congregation catches cold. It is your fault if the church steps are icy and somebody breaks his neck thereon. Of course it is not your fault, really and truly—but it will come to the same thing as if it were your fault; and do not forget this.

It will seem to be your fault if the organ, because of some pulmonary infirmity, breathes louder than it squawks—to borrow a reference Mark Twain made to his accordion. Why shouldn't you know something about the disorders to which an organ is prone? Now that the high altar has been supplanted by the organ, throughout practically all of non-conformity, that instrument, which occupies a position of such prominence, should be well known to you both as to its outer aspect and its internal mechanism.   If one of the Open Diapason pipes has contrived, by its measured vibrations, to jar loose a bit of art glass from the lead in a neighboring window, so that the glass rattles every time that pipe sounds, who has a better right to know exactly what to do about it than you?   If the "Swell to Great" plunger has gone on a strike, and the young lady organist is distressed about it, and it is Saturday afternoon— too late to send for an organ-repairer—why should you not be in possession of the knowledge that will enable you to put it right inside of three minutes?   You will be annoyed with the frequent indispositions of organs, all your professional life.   A knowledge of their habits and the ills to which they are most frequently subject, will often serve you well.

Let us return to the parsonage.   Your church is your landlord.   You are the tenant.   The fact that you pay no rent is beside the point in this discussion.   You pay no rent because your use of this house is part of your fixed income.   Therefore, the church is just as much a landlord and is under exactly the same obligation to you as if you were paying a rental to a stranger.   You are just as much a tenant and are under all the obligations of a tenant as if you were renting this house. If you never rented a house, and do not know what a tenant's obligations consist of, you should inquire of your lawyer friend for a lease, and study it. If you break a window, you must restore it. If you burn out your furnace grates, you must buy new ones. It is always understood that electric lamps are provided by the tenant, though all matters of wiring, fixtures, etc., are taken care of by the landlord. If you want floor-plugs, in addition to those already provided, that expense is on you. If the furnace is inadequate to heat the house, that expense is on them. See that they make you comfortable. You need have no more reluctance about asking for such things than you would if you were renting the property from disinterested outsiders, and paying rent for it. Sometimes your timidity to make a reasonable request, of this kind, is to be construed only as a confession of your precarious position in their esteem. If the roof leaks that is the church's business. Report the matter and it will be attended to promptly. They always fix leaky roofs, on record time, because there is an old tradition that water, running down through a house, is bad for the plastering.

If you should go to a church that has no parsonage, and have been successful in promoting a movement to build or buy one, you will find it to your advantage to locate it elsewhere than immediately adjacent to the church edifice. The parsonage, hard by the church, is well located as to sentimental considerations. Otherwise, it is a poor arrangement. To live beside the church means that you will be besieged, constantly, by a procession of agents, beggars, crooks, and leisurely persons who drop in to chat, on general principles. You are entirely too easy of access. If the parsonage is already located beside the church, you must live in it. If you have one to build or buy, take the advice of one who has tried it both ways—all ways— and reside a mile off. Unfortunately, too much of the minister's professional life gets milled up in his home life, anyway. The merchant leaves his store down-town, and goes home, in the evening, to dinner. His business is in one place and his home is in another. The doctor leaves his office, or the hospital, or the homes of his patients, and seeks his castle. He doesn't roll his pills in the kitchen, at home; nor does his family eat its meals off his operating-table, at the hospital. His family life and his professional life are distinct. If this were not so, the heavy exactions made upon him would drive him crazy. Too often, the minister is unable to distinguish between his professional and domestic pursuits. Unless he takes steps to avoid this, as much as possible, he will find, presently, that he has no home life at all.

Let us now do some thinking about the ways in which you may legitimately and dignifiedly supplement your income, which, so far as we have gone, is limited to your salary and your house. The question of fees for ministerial services deserves comment. There is, first, the wedding fee, which is, by custom, your wife's perquisite. Now and then a preacher will announce that he accepts no wedding fees. I cannot see what good may come of that policy. The bridegroom wants to do the customary thing by the minister who marries him; and, also by custom, the minister has a right to accept it. The preacher who refuses the wedding fee achieves little more than an embarrassment put upon the bridal party.

It is customary in some communities for the minister to issue a wedding certificate to the married pair. I have never done that voluntarily. If they insisted upon it I gave them a simple little printed blank, properly filled, which the bridegroom could stow away in his pocketbook. I have never kept on hand any of those ornate things that are to be framed and hung in the attic. My father (kindly forgive these frequent references to that good man) used to have three styles of wedding certificates in stock. A ten-dollar-and-up (it only rarely went up much higher) was entitled to a beautiful device, about seventeen by eleven in size, with nice little gold angels chasing one another around the margin, their arms full of flowers, and their clothes left at home. There were oval openings in the thing to contain the photographs of the principals and the pastor. My father's picture went along with this combination premium. For five-dollar weddings there was another certificate, not quite so expensive, bearing a picture of a wedding. It did not look like any of the weddings we ever had at our house in the old days, however. The bridegroom wore a frock coat, and the bride's veil was most impressive. Anything in the way of a fee, from a sum under five dollars on down to a basket of plums, was recognized by a certificate printed in plain black ink, which I always believed was the best worth having of the whole assortment. I do not know that this scheme was original with my father. I rather think it was not. Perhaps it was customary at that time in country "charges." Doubtless the neighbors could tell, without inquiring, almost exactly what one had paid for one's wife.

I do not accept baptismal fees, because I consider this service part of my business as a pastor for which I am being paid by the church. Once in a while, a father, trained in some denomination in which the baptismal fee is practically obligatory, has insisted upon handing me a dollar which I presented to the baby as a slight token of my regards. I do not accept

funeral fees. This is a debatable matter.
Many times situations will arise in which it
would be much less awkward, for all parties
concerned, if the fee were accepted. Now and
again your refusal of such a fee will only leave
the other man with a sense of an undischarged
obligation on his hands and, instead of improving your friendship, it will put your relations under a strange restraint. But in the
face of that occasional objection, I prefer to
keep my sympathy off the counter. It is not
a matter of whether they are able to pay you,
or how much. There is a principle involved,
quite apart from the dollars and cents. When
it is definitely known—as it speedily will be
known if you practise this policy—that you
accept no pay for funerals, your services, at an
hour when you may be of a great deal of comfort, will be much more valuable than if you
and they both knew that a settlement, in the
coin of the realm, is to follow later. Certain
exceptions may be made in the case of any
considerable outlay, on your part, in time or
travel, to attend a funeral in some other place
than your own community. Let them reimburse you for your expenses. This is only fair
to you and to them.

So much, then, for the fees accruing to the
minister in the course of his professional duties
—one fee, the wedding fee, and that his wife's
by right of tradition. But there are some in-

teresting by-products of your job which may as well be turned to profitable account. Every June should find you appearing, in surrounding communities, to speak at high-school commencements. Later in your experience invitations will come to you without any effort on your own part to secure them; but, for the present, you must exert yourself, somewhat, to make these engagements. Your ministerial dignity will suffer not a whit if you prepare a neat little folder, in early March, stating that Reverend I. B. Reddy, of Blinkton, will accept a few engagements to deliver commencement addresses, this season. You may print your cut on this folder, if so be that your face is an asset rather than a liability; and two or three brief press notices certifying that at the Odd Fellows' Anniversary you made the finest address ever heard in Pikeville. As the years pass you will have better clippings than this, wherewith to fetch your oratorical wares to market; but this one is good enough for the present. Secure the addresses of school superintendents and principals in towns near by, and mail your folders. Enclose a self-addressed postal card to encourage correspondence. You may receive a dozen queries out of fifty pieces of mail. The frugal ones will dislike to waste the postal card you sent them. You can write, stating your theme and terms. Don't lay it on too thick, at first, when you fix the tariff.

This avocation will become very profitable to
you as the years give you more experience;
but you cannot arrive unless you climb slowly.
It is much better for you, this first year, to have
three commencement dates at fifteen dollars
apiece, and railroad fare, than one engagement
at fifty. Be sure to get copies of the papers in
the towns where you speak. Press notices may
not mean much to the people who know exactly
what such tribute is worth; but it is to be observed that lecturers still depend mightily upon
them. You may be a very modest person, and
hesitate to promote your cause by these methods. If you will examine that kind of modesty,
you may discover that, in its last analysis, it is
the very last word in egotism. Well, it's all
up to you. If you would rather be dignifiedly
reticent about these things, there is no law
against it. If you wish to open a new avenue
of service—for I can't think of any more valuable message than that projected to a group
of adolescents on the occasion of their graduation—you will be obliged to get your start
through some judicious advertising. If my
own experience is of any interest to you, in this
connection, I am willing to tell you that I
began this high-school commencement business
in my first year out of the seminary, and have
never missed a season since; have had, in recent
years, as many as sixteen in a single season,
which is about all one can do in that line

through the brief period when such events are afoot. As your experience increases, your fees are better, naturally.

You need have no misgivings about taking this time away from your local work. Much of this effort comes back, in full measure, into your church's prosperity. The congregation takes a certain pride in the fact that their pastor is in demand for such service in other places. Not infrequently, some youth, at whose graduation you spoke, will come to your town to enter business. Perhaps you are the only man in that place to whom he will apply for friendship.

Then there are these luncheon clubs, meeting weekly, almost everywhere—Rotary, Lions, Kiwanis, Exchange, Civitans, Optimists, and a dozen more—in the market for after-dinner speeches. Except to seasoned speakers, who have won their spurs, these clubs do not ordinarily pay large fees, but they are willing to reimburse the unknown orator enough to be worth the bother. Make yourself known to these organizations, in neighboring towns; and slip away, occasionally, for a few hours, to fill such engagements. It will do you good. You will return to your job with fresh confidence. The experience of inspiring a group of business men—strangers to you—toward a higher type of thought and action, is going to be excellent training for you. The result of it will show up in your pulpit work. You will speak with more assurance and effectiveness.

While we are thinking about this matter, there should be called to your attention certain problems involved in such addresses (which you will deliver gratuitously, for the most part) in your own town. When you arrive in Blinkton, having finished a successful ministry in Pikeville, you will be amazed at the number of invitations you receive to speak for such organizations as those indicated above. And the Realtors will want you to talk to them, and the Merchants' Association; the D. A. R. and the G. A. R., the W. C. T. U., the Y. M. C. A., the Y. W. C. A., the Parent-Teachers' Club, and the Knights of This-that-and-the-other. Before you realize it, you will be repeating yourself, over and over, before groups which overlap, as to personnel; and it will become apparent that you haven't an unfired shot left in your locker.

Be careful, therefore, that in your eagerness to make friends for yourself and your church, you do not accept so many outside engagements that you are unable to fill them with credit to yourself and your cause. They will all think quite as well of you if you go into this business cautiously, spacing your engagements so that you have an opportunity, in the intervals, to work up some new material. And do not permit yourself to become too optimistic about the returns which may accrue to your work in the church through your speeches before these secular organizations. You may easily be deceived into the belief that the very excellent speech you made, at the annual "open-house night" of the Knights of the Gray Goose, will bring a large per cent of these gray geese out to your next Sunday morning's service. Be advised that very little of your extraparochial efforts, on the various local platforms and at club luncheon tables, will earn the reward you seek. If you are not on guard, you will discover that the very best work you are doing, in Blinkton, is performed before groups of strangers to whom you are not obligated, and from whom you need expect nothing whatsoever either in the coin of the realm or in later exhibition of interest in your pulpit ministry. Don't starve your own sheep while you offer the most succulent oratorical pasturage to these other flocks. Your first duty is owed to your own pulpit; and if you propose to scintillate, anywhere, do it there!

Moreover, this habit of accepting every invitation that comes along, to speak before every little club in town, is likely to have precisely the opposite effect upon your influence than the one you had hoped. It has a tendency to cheapen you and your message. In a few weeks, if you pursue that course, everybody in town will have heard you. Many will have heard you a half-dozen times. Some will have heard the same speech more than once, pleasantly introduced with the same good stories. You will soon be an old song. All curiosity concerning you will have been appeased. If you are wise, you will decline many more invitations than you accept, for the first six months; and when you do accept these invitations, go there prepared to offer something constructive. You will be expected to entertain, amuse, and instruct; and you can do all of these things without forgetting, for one moment, that you are a minister of the gospel. First, last, and all the time—you are a preacher!

Experience will convince you that much of the seed you scatter, in this manner, is tossed upon "the highway"—a hard macadam; but see that you sow it! Once in a while a grain bounces off into a bit of fertile soil. It might grow. But if you have a notion that you are doing valiant service for the kingdom, in divesting yourself of your best before these multitudinous secular societies, to the depletion of your pulpit power, you are laboring under a serious misapprehension.

Whatever may be the demand made upon you for public addresses, from the platform or at the club dinner-table, it is to be hoped that you will never arrive at that point of self-inflation where you have won the consent of your own mind to stand up and gabble. If your engagements multiply until you have reason to suspect that your oratorical disbursements are in excess of your intellectual income, you must either increase your income or pare down your expenses. Otherwise, you are in danger either of losing your own self-respect, or falling victim to a malady known to neurologists as "grandiose paranoia." I do not know which of these conditions is worse, but they are both bad enough to warrant your keeping clear of them.

It is easy to repeat the old speech; much easier than to go to the bother of preparing a new one. You cannot grow while the old is, in your opinion, good enough. Frequent bonfires of old addresses will be among your most valiant and judicious acts. If, during the early years of your professional career, you avail yourself of every hour of leisure, and spend that time in painstaking study and skilful literary composition, you may have occasion to rejoice, at fifty, that you laid adequate foundations for an effective pulpit and platform ministry.

The time will come when many duties and cares will crowd in upon you—accumulated responsibilities you could not even stagger under to-day. If you are successful, it will become increasingly difficult for you to secure uninterrupted blocks of time either for research or composition. So, the more successful you are planning to be later the more industrious you must be now, to learn to formulate your thoughts logically and to clothe them with vigorous and flawless rhetoric.

And this reminds me that there was a definite motion before the house—a little while ago—relating to the occasional address as a source of income. You may take some thought now for your pen as a lucrative instrument, if composition is easy for you.

I hesitate somewhat to speak to you about the business of writing for print. If I thought you were good for a long, tedious, disappointing experience in doing your level best, only to have your stuff come back to you, again and again, with a chilly little rejection slip enclosed, I could advise you, more heartily, to make this adventure. For the benefit of you who think you are up to that sort of misery, it may be said that here is a wide-open door. The world is fairly reeking with periodicals of all sorts. They must have copy. Somebody must furnish it. If you have anything interesting to say, with your typewriter, there is no reason why your right is not as good as some other's to help supply this demand. Of course you will be aware that a sermon has to be very, very extraordinary to win a place in a periodical that pays for articles. But there are plenty of topics which do not require homiletic treatment—matters of interest and profit. Perhaps you will wish to try your hand at this. If so, do not attempt to break in, at once, where the going is too discouraging. Do a little five-hundred-word essay for your local daily, now and then. Present it to the editor as a gift. Frequent publication of your articles will do you good in your church, and you will be gaining valuable experience in the art of composition. So far as I have been able to discover, the way to learn to write is to write. There are helps to be had, loaded with good suggestions. You should provide yourself with some of these books, if you expect to take up this matter seriously. But, after all has been said on that subject, you will learn the most you will ever know about composition by composing. Generally speaking, people write best about the things that interest them most. Young writers frequently waste their time and energy in writing of matters with which they are not fully conversant. There are two prime requisites to composition: first, you must have something to say; and, secondly, you must say it interestingly. If you are asked by your local editor for a sermon-abstract of five or six hundred words, take your manuscript (let it be hoped that whether you used it in the pulpit or not you did write it out in full), and discard the first seven pages as an initial move toward arriving at what the editor wants. Lead your sermon-essay with the most interesting sentence in the production. Include no "Let us, brethren," in your newspaper copy. The world is sick of that kind of lettuce. Indeed, the less of it that you administer from the pulpit, the more people will love you.

If your salary will not keep you, and you have been unable to supplement your income by any of the processes suggested above, you may be tempted, in an hour of emergency, to turn toward certain ways out of your dilemma which will do you small credit. You may resort to selling books, taking orders for magazines, or even pocket your pride completely and sell washing-machines, flivver accessories, and almost anything. Shortly before you arrive at the point where you have found that, in your case, the ministry as a profession is not economically sound, and that, in order to keep yourself going you must turn to the field of commerce, it is to be suggested that you go over to commerce wholly—lock, stock, and barrel—seeing you cannot do both of these things at the same time with any credit to either commerce or the ministry. To be selling anything whatsoever—no matter how little or for what—puts you into a position where your ministry cannot amount to much. It is to be regretted that this is true; for you might turn an honest penny that way. There is nothing wrong about selling real estate, bonds, coal, or potatoes. But you can't be a merchant and a minister! Either get out of the pulpit, or

away from the market-place! The two things
will not mix. Neither may your wife peddle
soap. If the ministry cannot provide you and
yours with a decent living, that is all the token
you should require as notification that you are
in the wrong line of business.

We must have some talk about disbursements. You cannot afford to be shabby. You
will be obliged to practise many economies; but
don't exercise all of your frugality in your
clothing. Doubtless you will not be able to
wear expensive clothes; but they should fit you,
and they must be kept pressed and in good repair. You have no right to wear a torn collar
or a ragged necktie.

When you set up housekeeping, it is better
to have a very few good things than eight
rooms full of cheap stuff that you will despise
and discard. Do not be too optimistic about
your ability to take care of a large number of
instalment purchases. Four dollars a month
for a set of books, and five dollars a month for
the vacuum cleaner, and ten dollars a month
for furniture, and twenty dollars a month for
the flivver totals a third of your wages, perhaps; albeit each item had seemed quite negotiable, considered separately.

You are a nomad. You are here to-day and
gone to-morrow. The men of your acquaintance chaff one another about their debts and
overdrafts. They sometimes talk about it as

if it were funny. It will not be so funny if you do it.

Carry all the life insurance you can afford. Begin to take it out as early as possible, to secure the lowest rates. Don't take any other kind of life insurance but that offered by the Presbyterian Ministers' Fund of Philadelphia, until you have your fifteen-thousand-dollar limit with them. Agents will try to persuade you that they can sell you safe and reliable insurance for as little or less cost than the company I have mentioned. But they are unable to prove it.

Do not dabble in stocks. You have no money to throw away. Any stock that is peddled among preachers, notoriously on their uppers, and more often than otherwise known to be incompetents in business, is almost sure to have something the matter with it. Be nearly as careful about buying bonds. They are always more readily negotiable, you will find, when you buy them than when you attempt to sell them. Four per cent in a savings-bank means more, in the long run, than eight per cent arrived at by some other process.

In conclusion, you should be made aware of the fact that although your salary will be increased, as the years pass, your expenses will jump up to meet it. Additional demands will be put upon you, every time your income rises. You will never be rich. Make up your mind to it, and find your happiness some other way.

And if ever you become curious to know exactly what kind of an institution hell is, accumulate a miscellaneous assortment of unpaid bills.

CHAPTER IV

MACHINERY

IT is barely possible you have been informed, at the theological school, concerning the structural organization of the church. If you are a non-conformist, you will probably have most of your dealings with two boards—the deacons and the trustees, or whatever is the equivalent of this in your denominational nomenclature. The personnel of the Board of Deacons may be somewhat similar to that of the Board of Trustees. Not infrequently, at the annual congregational meeting, men whose terms have just expired on the Board of Trustees, and are therefore ineligible to re-election, will be made members of the Board of Deacons, or vice versa. But you will discover that the mood and conduct of a deacons' meeting is quite different from a meeting of the trustees. At the deacons' meeting, the chairman opens the session by saying: "Brother Wilson, kindly lead us in a word of prayer." The trustees' meeting is formally in session when the chairman says: "Jim, pass the matches."

The deacons are supposed to attend to such matters as passing upon the qualifications of applicants who wish to unite with the church, and judgment upon the names of members whose disinterest has earned their release from that relationship. They advise on all matters pertaining to the religious services; supply the pulpit in the minister's absence with suitable clergy; look after the problems of parish relief; and counsel with the pastor on the problems of religious education. They are in charge of the sacrament of Holy Communion, as to its administration, and the upkeep and preparation of the equipment used in that rite.

The trustees attend to all matters of a prudential and fiscal nature; care for the property; prepare the budget; raise the money; pass on all questions of expenditure; execute all legal documents relative to church business.

You are expected to attend the deacons' meetings. The trustees will invite you in to their meetings when they want you. Don't try to make mere rubber stamps out of these official bodies. The more responsibility you put upon them the better they will serve you and the institution.

It is not very likely that your first work, or your second, will be in a church that can afford a Religious Education Director, to supervise the Sunday-school. This will be your responsibility. There will be a superintendent; but you will have much to say about the policies. The Women's Society will not need much more than your friendly interest and occasional word of appreciation. The women will like you just as well if you don't attempt to exercise too much leadership over them, in their society. Above all, do not permit yourself to be led into any sort of controversy with them over their own administrative procedure. If you find yourself longing for some kind of excitement, get a long pole and poke a big dent in the side of a yellow-jacket's nest; but let the women run their organization to suit themselves. They will do it properly; do not fear. The Men's Club is a difficult thing to keep in motion, as you will discover. The women can sew for the poor, knit for the Children's Home, bake and cook for the church's social affairs, and do all manner of dorcan (how do you like that?) philanthropies; but we men, in a similar organization under the auspices of the church, are but a bouquet of lilies who neither toil nor spin. The Men's Club can, and does, get together, occasionally, for a supper. Speeches are made, and everybody says we must get busy, now, and make this club amount to something. But it doesn't amount to much, and never will, unless there are specific errands and definite services laid upon its constituency. If you find that your Men's Club can be mauled into life about twice per annum, and that it spends the rest of the time in a coma, do not become so depressed over your failure that you take your own life. So far as I know, they are nearly all alike in that respect.

Men are going to spend just about so much time and energy in the church. You may be blessed with a really famous teacher for your men's class in the Sunday-school. He can get them out at nine-thirty on the first day of the week, in large numbers. He delivers an address which they enjoy, and which is about all they can hold for the present. So, when he is through with them, they are likely to go on home. If you are a better preacher than he is a teacher, you get them at ten-thirty, and he loses them at nine-thirty. But it is a safe wager that both of you can't succeed with this same crew.

If you are an organization specialist, you will be energizing the Busy Bees, Willing Workers, Knights of This-that-and-the-other, to the limit of your time and strength. Don't forget, while you are flying about on your little organizational errands, that the main power of your ministry does not lie in the machinery with which you surround yourself.

Speaking also of machinery, in another connotation, we must beware of placing too much reliance upon office fussiness. You and I belong to a profession that claims few tools for its proper performance. How I have envied the dentist the glittering and awesome trinkets of his trade! With what covetousness have I watched the doctor get out his blood-pressure thing (I fear it must have some other name than that among medical men)—his high-frequency machine, his cathode ray, his stethoscope, his various nickel-plated weapons! How I have wished, when entering a house to make a rather difficult call, that I might have at least the equivalent of a clinical thermometer to thrust under somebody's tongue, if for no better reason than that it would guarantee me a two minutes' start on the conversation! But, alas, we are of a toolless profession. When it comes to such matters, the barber has it all over us.

This leads me to say that the young preacher should get it firmly established in his consciousness that his business is not a desk job. Young Timothy Climber, in his first year at Waggles Crossing, sees visions and dreams dreams of a brighter day to come when, by pressing a button on his desk, he may summon into his presence an alert young woman with a stenographic notebook wherein to record his observations concerning the world in which he lives, and give utterance to the thoughts he would communicate to divers and sundry on his official stationery. The while he waits for this glorified hour to come, he beguiles the tedium of delay by surrounding himself with all the office machinery his modest income will provide. Filing cabinets, card indices, reference systems, and cross-reference systems, devices for the cataloguing of his one hundred and sixteen books, clipping drawers for the classified accommodation of his laborious scissors-work, letter-files, hourly ticklers, etc., to say nothing of parish maps, bristling with red, white, and blue headed pins to indicate the exact geographical location of the faithful, and complicated graphs showing his predecessor's administration to have been a season of drought compared to the jolly prosperity we are enjoying now. There's a funny thing about graphs. They are uniformly optimistic, and record gains so large as to make the beholder gasp. No graph, ever made by a minister, registers a loss.

You can get a nice little pocket record, for the use of ministers, in which the names of all your members may be written, with tabulations for the entry of calls made upon them. You will have a good time fussing with this little book. Go ahead and do it—once. You'll never be entirely satisfied until you have rigged one up for business. After you have experimented with it, you will content yourself, thereafter, with the card-index in which you keep the pastoral record of your constituency.

If young Timothy Climber is not on his guard against the danger of being wound up and milled through the gears of his own machinery, he will live to discover that it requires more time and ingenuity to fiddle with some of these office trinkets than their actual output justifies. To be sure, every young minister is to be pardoned for wanting to operate his institution "on a business basis." Just a bit envious of the precision and mechanical efficiency which he observes in his visit to the president of the tomato-can factory, where pushed buttons invoke clerks, and the walls are adorned with cabinets bearing classified and assorted information relative to the production and the market, this youth of high aims must be forgiven if he endeavors to conduct his own affairs with something of the same methodical accuracy. He even finds it pleasant to adopt the tomato-can-business lingo, and tries to think of himself as a manufacturer. He is a manufacturer of ideals, he says.

Now this is bad psychology. The minister is not a manufacturer, and the church is not a mill. This fact needs to be stated with emphasis, to-day. Many persons, completely carried away with the modern lust for the pragmatization of everything in the heavens above and the earth beneath, seem contented with the church's work in direct proportion to its ability to make a spectacular show of beehive activity. They are discouraged and exasperated if the church building is not in use seven days of the week, preferably working three shifts per day. It pains them to see the place ever closed up for an hour. To them, this is a heavy economic loss and waste. Huge property—they say—representing money into six figures, perhaps,

standing there, silent and useless, for so long
as a whole day. It worries them. The thing
should be working, working, working! There
should be a high column of black smoke belch-
ing from its chimney. People should be rushing about, inside, going through rapid motions,
and getting many things done! We will do
well to recover from this modern obsession that
the church is a factory. We must drop this
feverish, opportunistic notion that the church,
as an institution, must perform its errand in
the world, and render a report, by next Saturday! We must persuade ourselves that amid
all this hurry and worry and rush and scramble, for money, property, and pleasure, in
which most of our generation have been engaged until their nerves are ragged and their
minds distraught, it is of distinct advantage
that there shall be at least one institution left,
in this distracted world, which stands, dignifiedly and serenely, for a great, eternal fact!

Again, Timothy sometimes likes to think of
himself as a merchant—a salesman. He talks
of "selling" a new idea to the congregation, or
to the Board of Trustees. Time will cure him
of this habit. But if he would spare himself
the discomfort of arriving at this state of mind,
and going through it, and recovering from it,
he will do well to avoid it altogether. Commerce, these days, is not a very beautiful enterprise. Many men who are in the grip of its

ugliest problems, deeply appreciate an opportunity to forget about it, for an hour. Let the minister remember that he is not a merchant, and that his church is not a market. The stock phrases of commerce, adroitly filched from the lexicon of business, and woven into the prophet's conversation, add nothing to his ability in calling men's attention to the everlasting verities which undergird the life abundant.

This brings me to the point of saying that the successful minister, ardently as he may search for it and agonizingly as he may yearn for it, can never find a satisfactory mechanical substitute for close-up, hand-to-hand contacts with the individuals who comprise his parish. He will always be hoping, through the days of his novitiate, to find some ingenious desk accessory which will help solve this problem. To hunt for this invaluable article is a quest as unrewarding as the motorist's search for the fabled city of Detour, toward which he is directed, from time to time, but in which he never arrives. Timothy may write or type his parishioners' names, addresses, hobbies, aversions, specialties, talents, weaknesses; and the names of their children unto the third and fourth generation, upon five-by-three red cards, and copy them upon six-by-four blue cards, and draw maps of their places of residence, in relation to one another, so geometrically correct that they might be the envy of the Coast Survey—but unless he puts on his hat, and goes to see them, it profiteth him nothing!

He can bulletinize them and circularize them to his heart's content, and to the utter despair of the Finance Committee—but it will be as sounding brass or a tinkling cymbal if he makes no effort to become acquainted with them.

I, too, Timothy, have pooh-poohed the alleged necessity of ringing door-bells, afternoons, to inquire of people how they did, when the aroma of burning beans or scorching biscuits plainly certified that the visit was no less distressing to the caller than to the callee. Ourself when young did scorn a task enjoining a six-foot man to go about wasting his own and other people's time in such a manner. I think I have even gone to the length of saying it in print.

Any little group of preachers, in the privacy of a Monday-morning chat, will vote unanimously that the prophet Elisha, who probably first introduced the custom of parish visitation, bequeathed to his professional posterity a legacy of doubtful value. They call down anathemas upon the old fellow's bald head, and declare that pastoral calling is an unuseful drudgery. But, that afternoon, all but the doomed will turn out and demonstrate their willingness to be legatees of the bequest.

We are to have several chats, together, in this book, concerning this feature of our business. And before we settle down to the task of inspecting the details of it, perhaps a few general remarks are in order on the broad subject of the pastoral attitude. Maybe some of this talk belonged in Chapter I, where we were thinking about our vocation as a profession. If so, no matter. You belong to what might be called "an unprofessional profession," by which I mean that the more "professional" you are in your manner, as you pursue your daily activities, the less success you will record. Some vocations affect a uniform. This saves the persons engaged in such employment from the necessity of making themselves otherwise differentiated from the general public. The policeman doesn't have to swagger about with a menacing, bulldog expression on his face, to let the public know that he is in the business of keeping order. The doctor has his little bag o' tricks by which one inevitably knows him as a doctor. Probably most of the younger set of preachers, who may read these words, are not in uniform. I do not wish to be understood as holding the conventional ministerial garb in contempt. Indeed, there are many occasions when its usefulness so heavily outweighs its disadvantages that it is perhaps a toss-up whether it is better for the minister to button his waistcoat in front or behind. Personally, having tried it both ways, I am disposed to believe that if a minister does not happen to belong to a denomination which strongly recommends a clerical garb, his contacts with the public are more readily arrived at in the garments of the private citizen. The garb practically insures one against many petty annoyances. One does not hear so much profanity and rough talk. A gentle "Shush!" announces his arrival in the barber-shop, and requires the passing of certain cabalistic signs from one functionary to another when he drives into the public garage. There are some advantages in this, provided the uniformed clergyman does not run into situations where an insolent chap, of microcosmic mind and macrocosmic gall, wilfully plans his remarks to embarrass the man with the sacred label. All things considered, I'll wear a necktie.

In default of distinguishing marks to set forth their vocation, many ministers either consciously or unconsciously contract funny little habits of posture, accent, and carriage, obviously to indicate their line of business. Now if you have made up your mind that you are indifferent to your future success in the ministry; that you are entirely willing to be doing a grade of service not quite so exacting as that which you are potentially capable of—go to it, with all your ingenuity, and become just as affected and artificial as you wish, in your "ministerial" manner. If, however, you are ambitious to make something of yourself, in the ministry, and come at length into a position worthy of your latent ability, deal very severely with the first signs of a budding "ministerial" air. Watch yourself for queer little tricks of speech. Be on the alert to detect and squelch mannerisms. Above all, don't try to imitate some other man of your profession whom you hold in high regard! If ever your own personality is to have its chance, see that it is kept free of that bondage. Many a man is a mere mosaic composed of scraps and fragments copied from the personalities of others.

Some ministers may be easily identified as such by the fact that when they stop to speak to any one on the street, everybody passing by notes the oratorical inflection and wealth of gesture accompanying the great man's conversation. This type of minister always speaks "in public." He cannot even say "Good morning!" to you, in a crowded elevator, but everybody in the car cranes his neck to gaze upon the brother whose life-work is as thoroughly advertised as if he were a sandwich-man with his ecclesiastical pedigree on one board and the picture of his church on the other.

Just on the eve of falling into such disgusting habits, my young friend, take careful thought for the future. Put it down as a rule that the men of our profession who have contributed most mightily to the cause in which we are all concerned, kept themselves as "unprofessional" as possible. Don't—as you love your life—

affect any tricks which will make you conspicuous. When you distinguish yourself, achieve that end through the fineness of your service, rather than through the eccentricities of your manner.

A very commendable modesty and shyness, manifesting itself in self-consciousness, is likely to break out on you, like a rash, during your early experience as a public speaker. The fact that you are a youth, and your fear that people may be disinclined to listen respectfully and seriously to you, on that account, may put you into the habit of speaking, in public—and, presently, in private, too—with a different inflection, a different tone, than is yours by nature. Such habits are very easily formed, and they are hard to break. Indeed, they are practically impossible to break, once you have introduced yourself to the public in that manner. You can't very easily change your technic, after you have established it. I have heard preachers talk whose native state or country the most expert philologist could not have guessed. Indubitably there was a pronounced accent there, but exactly what it was—New England, Kentucky, Canadian, Welsh, Texas, or N'Yawk— might have baffled Sherlock Holmes. After you have listened to this sort of a fellow for a little while, you may conclude that this is Missouri, with a summer at Cambridge.

I have known young preachers—and old ones,

too—who seemed to be inordinately vain of a tremendous pile of unbarbered hair, though this observation may only be the ranting of a depraved jealousy in me who have been defended, by nature, against making such displays. Be careful you do not fall into the habit of shaking hands in a manner which implies a conferment of grace. You will do a great deal of hand-shaking, in the course of your life. Don't contract some trick here. Don't get into the habit of patting twelve-year-old boys on the head. Don't paw over people! Don't be so demonstrative with your affection, when you meet a man whose friendship you wish to elicit, that he is tempted to shout: "Down, Fido!"

The fact that you are more or less under observation, all the time, by virtue of your peculiar position, will make you extremely conscious of yourself until you become accustomed to the fact that you are living in a glass house. Of course the only sure cure for self-consciousness is an active and constant interest in other people. If you become sincerely concerned about them, you will forget about yourself.

So much has been said about the irksomeness of pastoral calling, the refined idiocy of the custom, the terrific burden it lays upon the shoulders of the minister, that there may be room for some remarks on the other side of the case. I maintain that this function of the minister may not only be relieved of its dulness, but made one of the chief sources of his happiness, if approached in the proper mood, and conducted according to certain fixed regulations, hereinafter to be set forth.

Let the weary parson, who has always believed that his pastoral ministrations were intended to be of benefit to his parish, divest himself of this idea altogether, and decide that when he goes out to make a call, he is going primarily to get something. For example: as he sets out to visit Auntie Grimes, who, because she is half-blind and bedridden, cannot gain much impression of the world outside, let him seek her in the capacity of beneficiary, rather than benefactor, eager to learn the latest deductions distilled in her spiritual laboratory. While he rushes about, attending committee meetings and conference lunches, distracted with innumerable trifling details—ninety-seven per cent of which come to nothing—this fine old soul has been experiencing an enforced monasticism, and has become a mystic. Here, for the asking, he may have, in thirty minutes, that which he has neither the time nor the patience to learn about the ways of God in a human soul —provided he goes for it as a humble seeker, rather than a noisy, puffy, back-slapping, handshaking professional pastor who rushes in, for a moment, to chuck Auntie under the chin and tell her she is ever so much better and looks like a rosy-faced high-school girl. Much as Auntie may appear to be appreciative of the fatuous compliment, and however cordial may be her expressions of delight over the fact that this great man had paused, in his flight, long enough to shout a few tempestuous nothings at her, she could give this fellow something that would add cubits to his spiritual stature if he had the wisdom and patience to seek her counsel, candidly admitting her to be his superior in matters of religious contemplation—which he probably could do without committing an outrage upon the truth.

When he goes into a house of mourning, it may be hoped that he carries some message of helpfulness; but if he enters there in the attitude of a suppliant, eager to learn what spiritual resources are vouchsafed the bereaved in an hour of grave emergency, and frankly lets it be known that he is there rather to get than to give, he will descend from that place much more of a prophet than when he arrived. It goes without saying that the grieving soul, approached in this manner, feels the necessity of summoning all the spiritual energy he possesses, to meet the demands laid upon him by his minister, who comes questing, rather than bestowing, that which makes humanity, in its gravest hours, rise to godlike proportions.

Every call, upon a parishioner, should have a definite errand affixed thereunto. You can elicit a promise from the lady that she will call, this week yet, upon the new people who moved recently into the next block. She has promised to report to you the result of that call. The pastor is to go about distributing responsibilities and commissions among the members of his congregation. Never is he to leave the impression behind him, as he departs, that he had come in the attitude of the policeman who rings headquarters, every half-hour, just to certify that he is still on the job, and earning his pay for walking the streets.

No office machinery will take care of this problem. Neither will any kind of auxiliary organization serve as a substitute. If the young minister thinks the time will ever come when he can handle all of his pastoral duties from his desk, in the church study, he is laboring under a delusion. True, the business of exercising pastoral care over a congregation numbering a thousand is an entirely different proposition than attending to the needs and wants of a church composed of one hundred and eighty-five; but if he expects, some day, to deal adequately with this larger task, his preparation for it will be made through the fidelity and resourcefulness with which he solves the problem now at hand.

CHAPTER V

VISITING THE SICK

IT is beyond hope that the minister should be informed of every case, in his parish, where his pastoral attention might be welcome. After he has done his best to keep himself aware of all the situations in which he is expected to manifest an interest, he will find that much of his pastoral duty is left undone for the very good reason that he has not heard of these cases in time to be of service.

Frequently it happens that his pastoral obligations will be quite heavy, at certain seasons; and it is with difficulty that he gives adequate attention to them all. In times when his schedule is crowded, he may be forced to leave some things undone. Whatever he proposes to slight, on such occasions, it must not be his visitation of the sick.

Almost any physical ailment involves a mental condition in which the patient is disposed to overrate his importance to himself and his friends. He has very little to think about besides himself, and he becomes extremely sensitive to any real or imagined indifference to his sorry plight as manifested on the part of his friends. Among the attentions which he con-

siders his rightful due, on this occasion, is a call
from his minister. Even if he has been most
casual in his attitude toward the church, and
neglectful of his religious obligations, he thinks
the church should show some concern about
his case, now that he has met an emergency.
He not only welcomes a call from the minister;
but, if it is not forthcoming promptly, he is disappointed. Consequently, the longer you post-
pone your visit to him, the harder it will be to
do him a service when you arrive there.

And if it should happen that, having been
informed on Sunday of the illness of this brother
—and he has been told that you are in possession of that fact—your other duties should de-
tain you from seeing him until Friday afternoon,
you may find him somewhat disposed to be
glum, a mood his household may share with
him. You may tell him of the large number
of people, at this season, who require attention
because of illness. This makes him part of an
invalided fraternity, and he feels less lonely.
You knew he was sick, and wanted to see him;
but knew, also, that he had enough understanding of your multiplicity of duties to wait, patiently, until you found time to come to him.
Whatever explanation you have to offer, for
your delay, let it be but one. A single alibi is
all you are permitted. To account for your
tardiness on the ground of a heavy programme,
your own indisposition, house guests who re-

quired attention, and a half-dozen other excuses, leads to his suspicion that you know yourself to be guilty of slighting him. Sick people have very active imaginations.

Every parish contains a small per cent of aged and infirm who need pastoral attention. Not only do they need it now, but they are going to need it so long as you both shall live. The young minister is informed, early in his residence in the new pastorate, that Grandma Brown would be delighted to see him. As a charter member of the congregation, Grandma has received much attention from the ministers, which she appreciates and well deserves. She is eighty, rheumatic, and lonely. She has been a long time ill, and has become adjusted to the fact that she is a permanent "shut-in." This, then, will be one of the earliest calls the new minister makes. His pastoral duties, at that time, will be limited by the fact of his slender knowledge of his field. Later, he will have his hands full. For the time, he is not so busy. So, he goes to see Grandma Brown; and he will be so cordially welcomed, and his recollection of his visit will be so pleasant, that, next week, he decides to repeat the experience—both for Grandma's sake and his own. Again he has such a good time that he resolves to be a frequent caller. For a month, he sees Grandma, punctually, every Monday afternoon. She remarks, appreciatively, about his "weekly en-

gagement" with her. This is their little joke.
Grandma hasn't received so much attention for
a long time; and, because her joys and expecta-
tions of life are limited, she counts on this
pleasure and comments upon it to the neighbors.

Soon, parish duties multiply. Whereas Grandma Brown was one of a very small group of people requiring ministerial attention, now Grandma belongs to an increasing host. The new
minister permits two weeks to slip by without seeing Grandma. She has confidently expected him; has called for her best lace cap;
has thought up a lot of things she wants to tell
him and ask him—and he has failed her. The
time comes when a whole month passes in
which she sees nothing of him. She wonders
whether he has found her less interesting than
he thought at first; or, has she said something
to wound him? Not having much else to think
about, as she sits all day long in her rocking-
chair, this problem may cause her a great deal
of anxiety. There is just a bit of humiliation
added thereunto, as she remembers how much
happiness she had experienced in telling her
neighbors of the frequent attention the new
minister was bestowing upon her. Are they
smiling about it? The moral of this episode is
that you must be careful about setting yourself
a regular task of periodical calling upon chronic
invalids. Don't give an exact periodicity to
these visits, at first, unless you are prepared to

see the enterprise through faithfully to the end; which may be a long contract.

While we happen to be thinking about the aged invalid, it should be observed that nature usually compounds her own subtle anæsthesia to numb the normal dread of death. You, at twenty-seven, contemplate death with such distaste that you imagine everybody else must feel the same way about it. You fancy your best contribution can be made at the point of attempting to distract attention from the thought of this mysterious warder of the exit gates of life. You do well to remember that, at seventy-five, the mind has been prepared for a calm and not altogether unwelcome consideration of the next step. This does not mean that you are to introduce the topic; but if your elderly parishioner seems inclined to discuss it with you, don't throw up both hands in horrified disavowal of his right to talk about such things. "Oh, my good friend, you mustn't be thinking about that!" you are prompted to say. "That will be a long time, yet!" Well, it may seem a long time yet from where you are; but the days of our age are threescore years and ten, according to an ancient adage; and, after that period has been spent, most people begin to be aware that they are not a very good risk, as the actuary would say.

Aged people do not wish to hear so much about the busy, bustling events of active life.

The report of these matters only isolates them, still further, from our mundane world, and confirms their annoying belief that they are unuseful residents in a place wherein their lease has expired. They do not greatly care what happened at the last church supper. It is of little concern to them that there is a new concrete walk in front of the parsonage, or that you have added a new stop to the organ. The fact that you exceeded your apportionment to missions, or failed of it, is of minor consequence.

The elderly Deacon Stone, when you inquire how he does to-day, may inform you that he is not long for this world. Believing that he should be wooed from this dismal state of mind, you are apt to think that your best service to the deacon is in beguiling his attention from his gloomy mood. You fairly smother him with a running commentary on current events, political movements, parish news, under the impression that you are rendering him a helpful courtesy. Quite to the contrary. If he wishes to talk to you about death, go to it with him, and talk as helpfully as you know how on this subject. He will, of course, know a great deal more about it than you do. He is nearer to it; more immediately concerned with it; heavily outranks you in experience and observation of it. That being the case, you have more to learn than teach in this interview; and your frank announcement that this is true will do much to clear the air for a conference in which both you and the deacon will be profited. The best talking you can do on the matter is by encouraging him to give you his own deductions. Sit attentively, at this hour, and give yourself a chance to learn something. But, however you may pursue this conversation, be sure that you pursue it. Do not evade it. If Deacon Stone has remarked that he is making ready to die, that doesn't mean that he wants to hear all about your trip to California. He wants you to hear about his projected trip to Glory. He is just as much interested in that journey as you are in the tour you hope to make to Europe, one of these days.

In his early experience of pastoral calling, the young minister has an instinctive dread of visiting, as a comparative stranger, in a home where some one is reported to be very ill. This feeling, on his part, is entirely commendable. For him to consider that situation in any other state of mind than this would mean that he has more brass than any young minister has a right to possess. But, whatever may be his reluctance to make such a call, he can assure himself, before he goes, that the members of the household will not regard him as an intruder. He has business there. He is not going as a private individual, but in his official capacity as the minister of the church.

Assuming that he is permitted to see the patient, he should remember that he is there primarily for that purpose—to see the patient. Two or three members of the family will accompany him into the room. They are "up and coming," physically; much easier to talk to than the patient, whose natural resources are at low ebb. He finds his line of least resistance proposing that he converse with them, across the bed, concerning the invalid. But he is not there to conduct a clinic. His attention should be almost entirely restricted to the patient. Sick people, you will discover, especially if they are not well known to you, are not to be depended upon to indulge in much sprightly conversation. Until experience has taught you how to manage a situation like this, keep a few general facts in mind, as follows:

In the first place, the minister must never prescribe. He is not the doctor. He must not assume to know anything about the treatment or care of this or any other malady. If he has any business there, at all, it relates to the patient's soul. He has not come to treat the body; and the more he chatters about the pathology of this case, the less confidence the patient will have in him as an expert in his own field. When the physician's name is mentioned, if he can with good conscience confirm the wisdom of their choice, he may deepen the patient's confidence in the doctor by expressing his own confidence in the medical man. Since the value of medical treatment depends, to a very large extent, upon the patient's absolute trust in his doctor, the minister's testimony to the physician's reputed skill is worth something.

If the case is very grave, the minister should not feel required to offer an unjustifiable hope of recovery by reciting what he believes to be similar cases which eventuated happily. It is to the minister's advantage to stand well in the regard of the physicians of his town; and if he gains the reputation of "a prescriber," or is known to talk glibly of therapeutic matters in every sick-room he visits, the doctors will consider him a poacher on their professional preserves.

Should the doctor arrive while you are making your call, courtesy and common sense enjoin you to leave; but you need not make such a hurried exit that the impression is left behind you your professional service is as nothing compared to his. To scramble out of a sick-room, under such circumstances, as if you were a mere neighbor, making a friendly call, is hardly fair to the cause you represent.

The minister's first business is to express his sympathy. In these days of professional nurses, the patient does not receive quite as much sympathy as in the old days when the members of the family took turns at the bedside. Doubtless this change is in the interest of progress. Beyond all question, many a patient has been fetched to an untimely grave by way of the well-intended compliance with his demands on the part of an affectionate household whose love was larger than their judgment. To-day, the nurse holds forth in magisterial manner. She is not there to sympathize; but to carry out the doctor's orders. Her job is not the most pleasant one in the whole wide world; but it has some compensations. One of these rewards is the abject obedience to her wishes, and servile deference to her skill, manifested toward her by the anxious members of a family that believes a great deal hangs upon her service. Having imputed to her a professional responsibility possibly quite out of proportion to her actual capacity to exercise it, she is apt to go about her business with the calm dispassion of a cobbler half-soling a boot. Sometimes she is icily matter of fact in her attitude toward the patient. The members of the family understand that the nurse knows her business thoroughly. They take their cues from her as to the best attitude to assume toward the object of their solicitude. The professional air of the nurse is often unwittingly imitated by the whole household. I have seen many cases where a curious constraint seemed to have laid hold upon the family. In the presence of the professional nurse—a stranger to them—they were shy and diffident. They wanted to express their love and concern by little words and gestures and tokens of endearment; but always this stiffly starched professional was standing by, thermometer in hand, trying to possess her soul in patience until this affectionate nonsense had been enacted.

I do not want to be misunderstood here as berating this profession. I have come into contact with large numbers of nurses whose fineness, every way considered, set them apart as superwomen, of whom the world is not worthy. But I have known, also, a considerable number of the other sort who, when they entered this vocation, obviously robbed the useful profession of dish-washing of a member in good and regular standing.

If the nurse has paralyzed the family's faculties for demonstrating affection, you will quickly sense the situation. Correct it by your own attitude in their presence. Your friendly admonition to the patient that he must "mind the doctor," and "obey the nurse," is to no purpose here. The invalid has heard little else but that manner of talk until he is pretty well fed up on it. He rather hopes you have come in with a new line of conversation. If the nurse has been autocratic, he has come to understand, subconsciously, that she is the barrier between him and the little amenities his family might naturally bestow. In such a situation, you accord her but little deference. She has had enough of that—probably more than is good for her. If you can manifest some honest-to-good-ness affection, here, your name will become immortal. It will be good for the family to see that the patient's hand can be held for two minutes, and patted, maybe, without his suffering a relapse. Let them understand, by your own attitude, that the nurse's presence does not deter you from saying some of the things that are welling up in their own hearts, and foolishly repressed for fear she might think them maud-linly sentimental.

Instead of saluting the nurse, as you enter the sick-room, with the doctor's conventional airy remark, "Well, how's your patient this morning?"—you do far better to dispose of her with a gracious nod, and approach the pa-tient at once, as if he had a right to be hailed with the second personal pronoun. He gets a good deal of attention that is phrased in the third person. When the doctor inquires about him of the nurse, the patient is in the third per-son. When the nurse replies, he is still third person. He has become a mere chattel. He is flat on his back, unable to refute the implica-tion that he is a lay figure. He has but little more to say about his case than if the occasion were an autopsy. The doctor thinks of him as "a typical pneumonia." To the nurse, he is "a case." The family, as has been observed, humors the mood of these professionals, upon whose skill so much depends, and themselves fall to talking about the patient as they would of any other natural object in disrepair. You can remedy this by making the patient the centre of interest.

Perhaps it is quite unnecessary to remark that the minister should not shake hands with sick people. Of course the patient will wish to do so. The minister is a hand-shaking functionary. Long custom demands that the invalid exert whatever energy he possesses to extend his right hand. You will have anticipated this. He knows he has it to go through, even if the business of shaking jars him terribly. But you will give him a pleasant surprise by extending your left hand. He does not feel required to shake your left hand. If you offer your right, he will try to shake it, probably to his discomfort. If you take his right hand in yours, and do not shake it, your greeting lacks something. So give him your left hand. He will not know why, and you need not tell him. He will be much better satisfied.

An affectionate hand that is laid upon his arm or his forehead, or that smooths his pillow, is going to mean more to him than any philosophy of comfort and serenity. If you are visiting a sick child, the gift of a simple little puzzle or a book of pictures is greatly appreciated. You need have no reticence about calling to see a mother of a new baby. The fact that she has given birth to a child certainly reflects no discredit upon her, nor is she any less entitled, on that account, to the attention of her minister. And while we happen to be on that subject, if her baby should die, aged six hours, you are to consider this as one of the most serious bereavements. Because of your inexperience of life's strange problems, you may think that a misfortune like this is quickly forgotten, and is of small importance. You will find it to be quite to the contrary.

You can talk of spiritual matters, in the sickroom, without directing the patient's attention to heaven. The kingdom is not restricted to "out yonder"; but is here, now, within you! The realm of the spirit is sufficiently broad to be talked about without invading the terra incognito whither our feet are tending. Unless the patient signifies his wish to discuss that matter, you do well to treat his mind as if he proposed to stay on here.

Whether the minister is to pray with the patient, or not, depends upon circumstances. If and when you do, make it as spontaneous as possible. If the prayer is addressed solely to God, it will be quite as effective if offered, later, in your own study. If, however, it is jointly addressed to God and the patient, both of these considerations must be kept in mind. I do not intend this to sound flippant. I am talking now about real facts; and I am trying to speak of them practically and honestly.

I have known cases where the patient was already sufficiently nervous about the outcome of his malady without having any more gravity imputed to it by the implication that he had now come to the point where the miraculous intervention of the divine is in order. If a prayer can be offered without unduly exciting the patient's alarm for himself, the minister may make a definite contribution here. It is much better to say, "Shall we offer a prayer together —you and I—for courage and strength?" than to suggest: "Would you like to have *me* say a prayer for *you*?" If prayer is offered, convince the patient that he is responsible for it, wants it, and is helping to present it. The best principles of mental suggestion should be employed in the phrasing of this petition. To begin by informing Deity that "our brother is in deep affliction" is bad psychology. God knows a great deal more about the plight of our brother than we; and our brother is probably quite obsessed by the thought of his "deep affliction." Steer clear of suggestions which inhibit his freedom of movement in attempting to rise above his aches and pains long enough to solicit spiritual power. Keep close to the hope-and-promise phraseology. The use of certain built-in passages of scripture, which have been of mental aid for ages, stating with certitude the rightful expectation of the believer that all is well with him, is of more benefit than any home-made comfort devised on the spot. Try to formulate your prayers so that when you are done, if you haven't helped him any, he is at least no worse off in mind than he was before.

It may come to pass that you will find your-self, some time, in the midst of a highly emo-tional, half-hysterical household, and some fran-tic member will beseech you to offer prayer. You will, of course, consent. There will be a general scurry to round up everybody in the house for this service. In the course of a mo-ment, you will be facing a very serious dilemma. If you begin your prayer under these conditions, almost anything you are likely to say will pro-duce an emotional storm. You must not take the risk of this. Beware of letting the situation get out of your control in this manner. After the family is assembled, you will do well to make them all a little talk calculated to calm their excitement and encourage them in their efforts to control their emotions. You can re-mind them that the fervent prayer of the right-eous availeth much, provided God is approached in faith. Prayer, to be effective, must pro-ceed from hearts sincerely believing in God's willingness and ability to help. "We must all render our friend this service, then, by pre-senting our petition with calm courage and resolute confidence." But don't go down on your knees to pray while a general emotional stampede is on, or impending. If you do so, you will wish afterward that you had been more thoughtful and deliberate.

Frequently, some member of the family follows the minister down-stairs, and converses with him, en route, in low tones. The patient hears this half-audible conversation, and decides that his pastor is now learning the worst, which had been previously concealed from him. Whatever the conversation may be, at such a moment, the preacher's contribution to it should be distinctly audible and unalarming. The patient may be disposed to forgive the doctor, and the nurse, and the family, for attempting to deceive him about his condition; but he likes to believe that the man of God is not in collusion with the rest of them in this disquieting intrigue.

If you have any doubt about your programme of talk with the patient, before you have seen him, ascertain exactly what the situation is before you enter his room. Sometimes the real nature of a disease has not been confided to the patient. There will be a fine chance for you here to make yourself about as popular as poison-ivy, if you make some disclosing remark to the invalid that lets the cat out of the bag. Very frequently, for example, a cerebral hemorrhage has been called by some other title than paralysis. The numbness of the right hand and right foot, and the slight impairment of speech, has been accounted for on the ground of general depletion of physical vitality which can be corrected presently through enforced rest and simple hygienic treatment. Your optimistic remark to the patient, therefore, that he can reasonably expect recovery inasmuch as your own best-beloved Auntie was paralyzed, just like this, and got back into things, in a few weeks, will nominate you, in that household, for a conspicuous place in the gallery of dunderheads. Find out, before you go into her room, whether the lady is really paralyzed, or is merely experiencing a strange neural condition which has suddenly dispossessed her of the use of one side of her body. If you have your own private ideas as to what ails her, you may store them alongside all your other private ideas—a department of your mental warehouse which will have to be enlarged, from time to time, to accommodate the business transacted there.

The length of your call is governed by conditions. If you are in a home where death is momentarily expected, you had better stay. The doctor does not linger long: there is nothing he can do. The nurse is obviously at the end of her resources; and signifies by her manner that her job is over. Nor is there anything much that you can do, except stay. It will not be a good time for you to remember another pressing engagement, much as you may wish to escape the experience of witnessing this heart-breaking scene. If you are required to remain until two o'clock in the morning, it is to be doubted if you can contrive a better use of your time. I look back upon a few such experiences, though terribly trying, as among the most useful hours of my ministry.

An accident has occurred, let us say, to some member of your congregation. You know that the family will be dreadfully upset. The conditions there will be tragic, in the extreme. You are timid about rushing there to offer your sympathy, and exercise the rights of your pastoral office. You would prefer waiting until tomorrow morning, when things may have calmed down a bit. But they need you a great deal worse to-night than they may to-morrow. Go at once! The more tragic it is, the quicker you are to arrive! The more harrowing the situation is, the longer you are to stay! The more anxious you are to escape, the more imperative it is that you remain on the job! This is important!

Hospitals have regular calling hours, usually from two to four in the afternoon. The staff will like the minister better and welcome him more cordially at the time designated for callers. He may think his profession gives him the right to ignore this regulation, as indeed it does in all emergency cases. But the physician makes his hospital calls in the morning, and the nurses are occupied with post-operative dressings, linen changes, etc., and do not like to be dis-

This observation is debatable. In the course of my own lifetime I have witnessed a marked change in the attitude of most people in regard to losses sustained by the death of their loved ones. It may be that the general broadening of our knowledge concerning the physical laws operative in our world has given larger encouragement to our belief that we are living in a universe from which there is no escape. Surely, we may speak with more confidence than ever before concerning the reality of those things which "eye hath not seen," now that wireless communication and the Roentgen ray are so common as to be taken for granted by the general public. If modern science should ever be disposed to attempt a defense of itself against the charge that it has proved to be subversive of faith in religion, doubtless it will point to the fact that its contribution to our thinking about the power and persistence of the unseen heavily outweighs the discomforts it has brought to the adherents of an unalterable orthodoxy.

But, whatever may be presumed to account for the fact that the majority of our people, to-day, face bereavement with more apparent understanding and control than so recently as three decades ago, it is a fact. I can distinctly remember when a violent emotional storm, at a funeral, was not the exception, but the rule. Only rarely does one witness such painful scenes, at this hour. Perhaps the present method of conducting the last rites for the departed may account for this change. But it is to be doubted if the improvement is to be credited to our profession. If there is to be any praise, let the undertakers have it.

Little by little, in the past few years, methods have been evolving toward a refinement of the funeral. Efforts have been made to soften some of its most cruel blows. When I was a lad, the funeral was practically a whole day's work. There was a brief service at the house; another, not so brief, at the church; a thoroughly heart-breaking service in the cemetery; concluding with the return of a large crowd of relatives, friends, and neighbors, to the bereaved home, "for refreshments." I used to drive the horse for my father, on many of these trips through the country; and there were stamped upon my plastic boy-mind certain harrowing sights and sounds which haunt me yet.

The science of embalming was in its infancy. The kindly disguises which now palliate, somewhat, the physical ravages of death, were then unknown. The little devices of recent days, invented to protect the bereaved from the ruder shocks incident to interment, were yet to come. Everybody saw it through, in all its naked terror; and custom decreed that no one might turn from it until the last lump of raw dirt had been patted into place by the deft shovels of the neighbors. Not much

wonder is it that the whole horrible enterprise
was customarily attended by such demonstra-
tions of the complete breakdown of all emotional discipline that I dread to recall it even
now when nearly all the other pictures, of the
same date, in my mental gallery, have faded
into an indistinguishable blur.

Gradually, the public has been educated, by
the undertakers, to think less and less about
the dirt part of it. Everything that genius and
sympathy might do to make mortality less hide-
ous has been done. But—let me repeat—the
undertakers deserve all the credit. We ministers have contributed very little toward the improvement. We still gloomily recite, as of yore:
"Man that is born of woman is of few days—
full of trouble—cometh forth as a flower—cut
down. Earth to earth—ashes to ashes—dust
to dust." Still pounding away on the old
"dirt concept"; still reciting that meaningless
remark, "Though after my skin worms destroy
this body, yet in my flesh shall I see God"—a
statement we take back, however, when we
call attention to Paul's declaration, "Flesh and
blood do not inherit the kingdom"—so there is
no actual harm done. The Pauline citation
neutralizes the remark of Job, and leaves everything very much as it was before; but oh, how
futile!

As I write these words, I have before me a
conventional funeral ritual. They are all very

much alike. Any criticism one might express in reference to this one may be equally predicated of all the others. I wonder how much good we think we are doing when we read, in a house of mourning: "When thou with rebukes dost chasten man for sin, thou makest his beauty to consume away, like as it were a moth fretting a garment." Exactly what—if anything—does that mean? Assuming that it once had some significance, what does it mean to-day, near the close of the first quarter of the twentieth century? Is it consonant with modern thought? And if so, is it in any way relevant to the matter at issue?

"Every man is therefore vanity," pursues the liturgy. Well, supposing that to be true— a very heavy and depressing charge against a race that thinks it has been redeemed; an indictment drawn up by a jaded old roué whose career quite disqualified him as a counsellor to normal people—supposing it to be true, which it isn't, what of it? Does this ease the pain, in the slightest degree?

"Thou turnest man to destruction," continues the liturgy. Personally, I do not believe it; but assuming, for sake of argument, that it is a fact, what is the good of saying it to a little group of weeping people who are all bundled up for their drive to the cemetery, where they expect to bury the remains of their Harry, or Grace, or mother, or daddy? "For we consume away in thy displeasure, and are afraid at thy wrathful indignation." A fine piece of consolation—that.

Obviously it is high time we gave ourselves to some serious thinking about the ways and means whereby we may offer a larger contribution to the distressed. Surely, it is not for lack of consolatory scripture that we have failed to do better in our ministry to the bereaved. Long since, I have left off reading the gloomy requial verses which postulate the severity of The Absolute, and explain death as an act of judgment.

Experience has persuaded me that the most satisfactory funeral service, in these days when the chief request is a plea for brevity and simplicity, is a synthetic scripture reading compiled from the Twenty-third Psalm, selected verses from the fourteenth chapter of St. John, and a few sentences from the fifteenth chapter of First Corinthians, followed by a prayer, and a ten-minute address on the general theme of the Life Everlasting. Unless the decedent is a person in public position, I rarely refer to his personal characteristics, except in the most general way.

As the officiating minister, at a funeral service, you may safely assume: first, that the persons in attendance know as much as yourself about the virtues of the departed—perhaps a great deal more. Indeed, in many cases it would be but little short of an impertinence for you, a comparative stranger, to indulge in eulogy in the presence of a group wherein you are the least informed, of all of them, concerning the tender matters of which you speak. You may assume, in the second place, that the family is thoroughly aware of the loss that has been sustained, and requires no advice from you serving to deepen that conviction. You are there to offer consolation.

After experimenting with a variety of programmes, I have found that the following ideas seem to afford the most comfort. I am passing them along to you, in a very brief and sketchy outline. I am in Maeterlinck's debt for the thought that if an unborn child could reason, he might contemplate, with horror and alarm, the fact that he was presently to be driven forth from the maternal warmth and security into a world of illness, accident, care, and labor; but, having made adventure in that new world, on no account could he tolerate the thought of a return to his earlier state of living. But, now, with even more apprehension, he attempts to avert his eyes from the fact that he is presently to be transferred into still another mode of life—probably as much less limited as his present state of existence is less limited than his prenatal life.

The truth that the idea of survival is a universal belief, belonging to all ages, all countries

—confessed with equal fervor and confidence by savage and sage—is a consoling thought. Doctor Fosdick has offered some help in his statement: "Were we to live by the appearances of things, we should spend our lives in ignorance of the most important facts in our world." To our senses, it seems that our friends are gone. But "the best knowledge we have is arrived at through the utter repudiation of certain testimony based upon appearances. Our earth appears to be flat; but it is round. At noon, the stars appear to have left the sky; but they are all there." We need only be plunged into the depths of an enveloping darkness, to discover how brightly the stars are shining. "All human knowledge has been won through a criticism of our senses, by going back of the way things look to the way things are. Physical sight reports that a man grows smaller as he recedes into the distance; insight says that he does not. Sight says that death destroys," leaving nothing but an impassive semblance of one's friend. "Insight declares that the life is more superior to the body than the body is superior to its raiment."

Some time, when you have a little child to lay away, read Leigh Hunt's essay on "The Death of Little Children" before you prepare your address. If you are called upon to speak at the funeral of one suddenly taken, in the midst of an active career, it will be helpful to remind the friends of the departed that there are two aspects to immortality—the immortality of the soul Over There, and the persistence of his influence here. If they are disposed to be affectionately rebellious over the fact of his obviously unfinished work, it is quite within their power to give him added years, here, by redoubling their own interest and energy in promoting the causes to which he had given himself with such zeal.

Before you have spent a decade in the ministry, you will have discovered that bewildered people, passing through the Valley of the Shadow, are sometimes moved to make strange requests relative to the conduct of a funeral service in their home. You should comply with these requests, in so far as you are able, even though they involve curious procedure which you would never have thought of yourself. Remember that at such times people's minds are badly upset. Perhaps you have never passed through a serious bereavement. If not, you cannot be expected to understand; but you may take their word for it who have suffered— this is a time when nobody is exactly normal.

You will be asked to read verses, written for the occasion by Aunt Emma. The poem may be longer than deep; no two lines of it may be of the same school of poetic architecture; the sentiment may be even more strange than the garments wherewith it is clothed. But you will read the poem by Aunt Emma. Tinker it up, and read it as impressively as possible. However crude it may sound to you, it may be the most satisfying part of the service, because Aunt Emma wrote it. Your pride may suffer, somewhat, for you have been instructed not to divulge the secret of its origin. Many people there will think it your own composition, and wonder what could possibly have led you to do it. On no other occasion, in the pursuance of his vocation, is a minister more likely to be confronted with the necessity of being "a fool for Christ's sake."

Not infrequently, extended biographical matter will be provided for you to read at the service. Read anything they think they want read. I once spent a full twenty minutes reading newspaper clippings concerning a man who, as Prosecuting Attorney, had sent more people to jail than any other person who had ever occupied that position in his county. It was the highest tribute that could be paid to his efficiency as a public servant, and they wanted it read. I read it. Had I been left to my own devices, I should have been reluctant to direct him to the throne of mercy with these credentials; but it was not mine to reason why.

When a death is reported to the minister, he should go to the home at his earliest opportunity. Even if the message comes to him with all the facts he needs to know, he must go to the house, anyway. If the deceased is a member of another church than his, but certain members of the household are of his congregation, he should attend the funeral, if possible, and be quite as attentive, both before and after the event, as if he had been asked to conduct the service.

Occasionally, a death will occur in some family of your congregation whose members have been intimately attached to your predecessor. Conversation will develop the fact that they wish this minister might be present. Here is a chance for you to show everybody in your parish what sort you are. Many a sprightly scrap has been staged, and many hard feelings engendered, by the return of a prophet to his erstwhile parish for the purpose of offering consolation to his old friends. The preacher who is so jealous of his "professional rights" that he attempts to enforce them at an hour when people aren't thinking clearly, or pausing to reflect upon how anybody else might feel about this, except themselves, should be in some line of endeavor less exacting of a Christian character.

Consent, cheerfully, to this arrangement. At the first hint of this desire, on the part of the family, take the initiative in planning for its execution. Wire the other minister your own hope that he will come. Meet him at the train. Extend him every courtesy. If, at the last minute, you are asked to take some minor part in the service, do whatever is requested of you. The minister who lacks the magnitude of mind to go through an occasional experience like this without showing himself aggrieved has no right to belong to our profession.

Customarily the funeral is held at the family residence. In my opinion, the proper place for it is in the church—a church whose appointments permit the family to have privacy from the mere business acquaintances and neighbors by being seated in a little adjoining room where they may hear and see unobserved. The ideal service should be a triumphant expression of faith. A trained and competent choir should be on duty, perhaps opening the service with a stirring rendition of Gounod's "Unfold, Ye Portals." We might contrive to do some good if we had people educated to this idea. But that, I dare say, is beyond hope. The funeral is held at the house. You will arrive five minutes before the service. There is little you can do with the remaining time, except be conscious of the fact that you are more or less in the way of the arriving friends, who must walk over you as you sit where a chair has been placed for you. This is a good time to slip up-stairs and have a quiet word with these sorry people. Perhaps you will wish to offer a brief prayer with them, in the intimacy of this family circle. Maybe there will be no opportunity for that.

If not, a hand-clasp; an affectionate pat on the shoulder; a word inspiring them to courage—you may decide, later, that you did more for them, in that moment, than through the service you read at the foot of the stairs.

It is no longer considered imperative that the minister walk bareheaded, on a winter day, from the door of the house to the door of the hearse, or from the hearse to the grave. Pneumonia is a very high price to pay for the conventional tribute of respect involved in that exposure. I shall not do my late friend's memory the discredit of thinking that he would be pleased over my taking such a risk. When the minister has the good judgment to leave his hat on, the pall-bearers and others follow his example.

The undertaker is always anxious to get everybody away from the grave at the earliest possible moment, after the committal service; and this is entirely right. The minister can easily manage, however, to walk back to the coach with the next of kin, and show his comradeship in this most trying moment of all. For him to turn directly from the grave, after the benediction, and go his way to his car, without a word, seems a bit chilly and perfunctory.

Not much time should elapse after the funeral until the minister calls on the family. Frequently I have gone there directly from the cemetery, on occasions when some one in the household seemed close to the breaking-point. When you make your post-funeral call, you may offer some helpful counsel on the subject of their new obligations; the importance of rapidly reconstructing the life of the house to meet the changed conditions; the danger of brooding in seclusion; and the inevitable disappointment of all who travel "the way to Endor." Perhaps some well-meaning neighbor, who once tinkered with an ouija-board or attended a séance, has already stirred their curiosity concerning spiritualism. If she hasn't yet, she will. You may safely act on the assumption that this is a good time to discourage any attempted communication with a world from which we are separated for the sake of our own peace of mind. You can assure them that if we knew of the life they now live, who have been transported to celestial happiness, we might find our present tasks unendurable. A few timely words on this subject may divert their attention from a programme brimming with mental misery.

Find time to keep very close to these people, for a while. Every time you are in their part of town, for a few weeks, drop in, if only for a moment. This not only helps the bereaved family; it helps the minister, also. He needs to know how other people behave under fire. Sometimes, when I see the magnificent way in which men and women rise to meet the blow, and the splendid manner in which they exercise their faith and courage, after they have had the dearest thing in life taken from them, it makes me proud to feel that I am a member of the same race to which they belong. It does no harm to tell them so.

CHAPTER VII

FOR BETTER, FOR WORSE

THE only ministerial function you will perform under the joint authorization of Church and State is the wedding ceremony. It is not enough that you are an ordained minister; your credentials must be approved by the County Clerk, the Probate Judge, or whatever civil authority passes upon such matters in your State. The laws governing this are not uniform in all the States. Inform yourself on this point before attempting to perform a wedding ceremony, or you may find yourself with an awkward situation on your hands.

You will have been told, in the theological seminary, that the wedding should be made an impressive and dignified event. This was good counsel they gave you. The fact that marriage is not a sacrament, in the opinion of Protestantism, does not excuse our frequent attitude of nonchalance in administering a rite which should never be celebrated or received otherwise than "soberly, advisedly, discreetly, and in the fear of God." Persons who object to the Roman dogma which hallows this ceremony to the extent of giving it sacramental value should pause, on the verge of a polemic outburst, and examine the comparative statistics which disclose how very much better is the Catholic than the Protestant record of faithfulness to wedding vows. This points a moral. It indicates that the more impressively solemn this rite is made, the better are the chances of its permanent value. In these days of startlingly depressing reports from the Court of Domestic Relations, any procedure which may be presumed to dignify matrimony, and deepen the significance of the obligations involved, deserves the respectful attention of all men empowered to perform this service.

Notwithstanding the fact that your instructors, in the seminary, did their best to impress you with the responsibility imputed to you, as indicated above, it is doubtful if they told you much about the actual technic of the wedding. The procedure of it you may have to learn in the rough school of experience. It is entirely possible that at your first wedding you did not know enough about the enterprise to be able to instruct the lucky fellow which side of his bride he should stand on. I distinctly recall the curious questions addressed to me on the occasion of the first rehearsal I ever attended, in the capacity of officiating clergyman, prefatory to a church wedding of much pomp and circumstance; and how I wished, that night, I might be able to swap all that I knew about

the Minor Prophets for a ten-minute chat with
somebody who knew all about weddings.

Let me speak first about the impromptu
wedding that drops in on you, at the parsonage, or at your church office, unannounced.
These people, unattached in any way to you
or your institution—merely bobbing up from
nowhere—are not always treated with quite so
much consideration as they deserve. These
cases, instead of being handled with "a lick
and a promise," require all the attention you
can give them. You are warranted in having
a five-minute chat with them, previous to the
service, in which you put them at their ease,
and win their friendship. Never send a wedded
pair of strange people away with the feeling
that they and their affair meant nothing to
you beyond the fee. While you are engaged
in the necessary clerical work on their marriage
certificate, let them understand that you are
interested in their future happiness. Don't go
through this operation mechanically, as if you
were signing the receipt of a telegram. Find
out where they are going to live. Make an
effort to keep track of them, later.

Probably most of the weddings at which you
officiate will be held at the home of the bride.
Even if it is to be a very simple affair, the principals will be glad to have a little talk with you
on the day before the wedding. They should
be assured that you will not permit them to

make any awkward blunders. Recite for them the important phases of the ritual you propose to use. Remember that while this is "all in the day's work," so far as you are concerned, it is the greatest moment of their lives, thus far. Humor them if they seem more fussy than necessary over the minor details of the pageant.

You should gather all the information you can lay hold upon, anent the technic of weddings. When rehearsals are held, you will be asked many questions. It is impossible, of course, to expand here upon every conceivable situation; but a typical case, or two, may be cited to advantage. Here is, for example, the impending marriage of Edith, the only child, who, her father declares, "by Jingo, is going to have a wedding that'll knock 'em cold!" It is to be a home wedding, but there will be a hundred and fifty guests; lots of out-of-town people; a hired caterer, a hired director of pageantry, a hired orchestra; and all the rest of the trimmings—regardless of expense. At the last minute, however, when the rehearsal is going through its preliminary skirmishes, in the midst of violent confusion, Aunt Effie will arrive from New Orleans, and the hired director of ceremonies will have a four-dimensional problem on her hands. Aunt Effie will take a few tucks in the procession, object to the height of the floral altar, move the candelabra away from the "chancel" to decrease the fire risk, and protest against having the maid of honor start, from the head of the stairs, when the orchestra plays "Tum, tee-tee, tum"—deeming it much better to wait until the passage "Tee, tum-tee-aye-tum-tee-tee"—which just brings everything out right, at the altar, don't you know.

After this debate has successively passed through the various stages of excessive polite-ness, oh-but-my-dear-ing, dignified hauteur, dangerously suppressed exasperation, thinly veiled contempt, frank exchange of personal insults, and is rapidly approaching imminent physical combat, Edith's hysterical mother will beam brightly with an inspiration! She won-ders why nobody had thought of it before! They will put it up to you to decide whether the will of Aunt Effie or Madame Etta Quette shall prevail!

Frequently, in pursuit of your vocation, you will be elected the official goat, by acclamation, on occasions apparently demanding your sub-missive acceptance of the distinction; but here, if I were you, I should gracefully decline the office. At such a moment, you should be able to recall that you wish to see the principals, alone, for a little while, to tell them what they should know about the ritual. Perhaps, while you and they are gone, the racket may be arbi-trated.

It is unwise, I think, to attempt any of the wedding service, at rehearsals, in the presence of the relatives and friends. This rehearsal is mostly for the purpose of organizing the bridal procession so that all parties to it will know exactly what is expected of them. You should talk to the principals about the ritual, and ask the immediate attendants of the pair into your conference when the ring business is discussed. You will find young people quite apprehensive about the ring. They are going to fumble it, they think, and drop it. I never saw a ring dropped; but I have rarely prepared a couple for a wedding when this fear was not expressed. Once, the three-year-old ring-bearer, tiring of the event, and remembering something else she wished to do, ducked out, between the pair who were in the process of becoming one, and was in a fair way to put a crimp into further proceedings. Bystanders rescued the ring, and permitted Flossie to go about her other affairs. Since that time, I am always anxious when the baby niece is invited to carry the ring.

You may easily relieve all anxiety about dropping the ring. If the ring-bearer is present, she hands the ring to the best man. If she carries it in a rose, she simply holds up the rose and he takes the ring in his fingers. Or, if there is no ring-bearer, the best man has it in his pocket. In any event, then, he takes it from the rose, or from his pocket, with his fingers. He places the ring in the bridegroom's open palm. The bridegroom does not touch the ring with his fingers, but offers it to his bride, who takes it from his palm with her fingers and places it in the minister's palm, or upon his book. Now the bridegroom takes the ring in his fingers, and places it upon his bride's hand. In this manner—transferring the ring from fingers to palm, palm to fingers, fingers to palm—the chance of a blunder is avoided, and the fear of a blunder is dispelled. This may sound like a very trivial matter; but you will have set many a nervous fear at rest by such little suggestions which indicate that you know what you are about, and are not likely to permit them to make themselves ridiculous before their friends.

We will suppose that the home wedding is to be conducted without quite so much fuss as Edith's. You will be asked to furnish advice concerning the order of events—seeing there is no hired director of ceremonies. You should be prepared to do so; ready, however, to comply instantly with the wishes of the household, should they fail to coincide with yours. It is very simple. The bride and her father—if she has one—are up-stairs. So are all of her own attendants, be they few or many. The bridegroom and the best man are out in the butler's pantry, or tucked away somewhere else, down-stairs. When it comes to the actual wedding, you will be there with these men—wherever they are. At the rehearsal, if you are giving advice, you will only pretend to be with the bridegroom. You will stand at the improvised altar, offering suggestions. Ribbons will be stretched, probably by the ushers, or juvenile members of the household, about two minutes before the procession starts, indicating the line of march. Whatever manner of music is used, the conventional wedding-march will no more than conclude its opening measures than the minister leaves his place with the men, in the kitchen, and moves slowly toward the altar, followed, at a distance of ten feet, by the best man and the bridegroom, the latter walking to the left of his attendant. The minister is not to come galloping in, making no endeavor to keep step with the music. He is not to signify, by his attitude, that he is willing to go through all this flummery, just to please their caprice; but, as anybody can see, he considers it rather silly. He is not to stay out in the parlors and chat with arriving guests, up to the last minute, and make his way to the altar, hastily, when he sees the bridal party approaching. Many a minister, seeming, out of his greatness, to disdain the petty pomp of such an occasion, is pronounced a very dull fellow by the audience. If he thinks thus to create the impression that he is quite too important to be made conformable to the little details of this event, he only surprises the cultured persons present with his gaucherie.

When the men start toward the altar, the
signal is passed, by some one charged to do so,
to the people up-stairs. The best man and
the bridegroom will have arrived at the altar,
and are waiting, before any of the ladies appear. These gentlemen are, at best, only lay
figures; and should have their performance all
out of the way before the really important per-
sonages show up. Equally spaced, in the line
of march, are the various members of the bridal
train. In this particular party, we will say
that the first to appear is Gladys, our little
niece, six years old, bearing the ring. Next
comes sister Maud, as maid of honor, and
finally, side by side, come the bride and papa
—the elder on the right. Papa will have been
dragged into this affair by brute strength.
And now that he has reluctantly consented to
it, the task imputed to him is giving this good
man a great deal more worry than the cause
seems to justify. It isn't a bad idea to have a
few minutes with him, in the library, after the
rehearsal, reciting to him the valiant deeds of
his friends Messrs. Smith, Jones, and Robinson,
who, under compulsion to do this same thing,
against their several wills and accords, distin-
guished themselves with great credit. If papa
doesn't buck up, after having his heroism thus
challenged, try reconciling him to it with the
solemn reminder that it is our common lot.
Anyway, he ought to feel complimented that

Susie wants him to do it for her. Suppose she did not want him! How would he feel about that? But, don't neglect the old chap, utterly, or appear unmindful of his misery; for his is a difficult rôle to play. He ages under it markedly. He fairly totters under the weight of the years which his part in the affair imputes to him. Moreover, he has a dangerous piece to say, in the ritual, inasmuch as it consists of only two words, which hardly gives him a sporting chance to retrieve himself, in case of error. To stumble on a single syllable means that he got half of his part wrong. Be gentle with papa.

Well, let us assume that you are at the altar and all the figures in the picture are properly placed. If there are ushers, they will have taken their place at the right end of the line, perhaps. Much of this is subject to the local conditions. The persons immediately before you, not counting the other attendants than the best man, papa, and the maid of honor, are, in the order of their standing—from your left to right—the best man, the bridegroom, the bride's father, the bride, her maid of honor. The ring-bearer is directly in front of the best man, or slightly to his right.

Do not begin the service until the figures are all properly in line about the altar; and do not hurry the ritual. This service is to be read with dignity; not in the sepulchral tones of the committal service; but certainly not with the chatty informality of an after-dinner speech at the Rotary Club. Take your time. Make it impressive.

Probably no wedding was ever yet conducted, to which the participants had looked forward with any degree of interest and careful planning, wherein the minister was not previously charged to make the service "just as brief and simple as possible." You will be instructed, occasionally, that "we do not want any lines to say, in the ceremony." You are entirely justified in telling them candidly that if they think you don't know how to perform a wedding ceremony, they are at liberty to employ some one with higher credentials. For these people to inform you how to perform this rite is an impertinence. It is no less impudent than for the patient to give his surgeon orders as to the exact amount of time he may devote to the excision of his liver. When any callow youth of twenty-three comes to me with sage counsel about his wedding service—instructing me how it is to be performed—he invariably learns something new and interesting about the courtesies due a professional man, touching the matters with which he is presumed to have special knowledge.

Presently, in the service, papa will fade out of the picture. You have asked "Who giveth this woman?"—and papa has uttered his two significant words. That is the end of him. He steps back to rejoin mamma, who is close enough at hand to permit this without too much tramping around. The party tightens up, now, to close the breach caused by the loss of papa; and things proceed. The more instruction these people have, in advance, and the less stage direction they require, in the course of the service, the more impressive it will be. When you have arrived at the ring business, it is not necessary for you to call for that property audibly. A significant gesture of your left hand, toward the ring-bearer, barely noticeable by any besides herself, will set all that matter in motion. If there are two rings, the maid of honor has the one the bride proposes to give to her husband. The bride slips it on his hand when she recites the words whereby she gives him her troth. Whether this ring is to describe the circle, in the manner of the bridegroom's ring, is a matter of option. It is much more impressive—because more simple—if the bride's gift to her husband does not travel about from hand to hand, but is given her by her attendant, and placed upon her husband's hand, by herself, during her formal recitation of the lines mentioned above.

Now that we happen to be talking about the wedding ritual, you will probably decide, after you have experimented with some of the other forms, to settle down on the Episcopal service, perhaps with slight modifications, as the finest and fittest of the lot.   It is dignified, impressive, not too long, not too short, carries conviction, and has the advantage of being a historic document.

Once in a long while, a wedding goes forward without a ring.   The bride considers it a badge of servitude, and will not have it.   You are to govern yourself accordingly.   If she doesn't want it, it is none of your affair.   Whenever the ring is used, however, the service which accompanies it should be employed, exactly as it stands in the book.   The "worldly goods" which he assigns to her may be purely hypothetical; but it is the spirit of the thing that you are after.   Once I was marrying a man to a woman who had all the money, and he insisted upon saying: "With all thy worldly goods I thee endow!"—and seeing he was speaking words of truth and soberness, albeit not exactly according to rote, I let it stand at that.   A good story is told of a young medical student who, in venturing upon matrimony, had brought nothing to his bride but a very bright future. A few of his student friends were asked in to honor the event; and when he recited the conventional line, "With all my worldly goods I thee endow," one of the young students whispered to his mate: "There goes his bicycle!"

In the episode of the "plighting of troth," do not say to the bridegroom, "I—with your name," for, in his nervousness, he may repeat exactly what you have said to him—"I, with your name." I have heard them do it. Say, rather: "I, John, take thee, Mary." Always use Christian names. If unacquainted with these people, ascertain, before you go into the service, by which of their names they are known best. Do not ask Mephistopheles Gabriel Jones, who has been signing his name "M. Gabriel Jones" all his life until, in the stress of that inquisition at the court-house, he betrayed his secret—do not ask him to say: "I, Mephistopheles, take thee, Margaret." Find out if he isn't Gabriel to his friends.

Avoid all these nice little "folksy" ceremonies, which begin with some syrupy stuff about the cute little nest these birdies are going out to build on a neighboring bough—mere silly saccharine slush, wallowing in the sentimentality of sentiment. You will find that all of these home-brewed rituals lack a great deal of the dignity, power, and charm of the service to which I have referred. If you are bent upon using something that you made at your own homiletic work-bench, try to render it as impressively as possible. The wide handicap you have accepted will make it important that you should put the best of your personality into it. Of course even the Episcopal service can be read in a tone that lulls into trances those whom it does not anæsthetize; but I think you will find this the most nearly fool-proof of all the ceremonies by which this rite may be celebrated.

When the service is ended, the bride has to be kissed by her husband. Later, she will be pawed over by the assembled multitude. You may kiss the bride yourself, if she and her family are well known to you. Whatever system you adopt, apropos of this matter, and in respect to your own case, you would better adhere to it, or you may some time let yourself in for the criticism that an occasional bride is, in your opinion, hardly worth the bother. At all events, the bride is to be kissed by her husband. You will confer a favor upon these young people by telling them what is to be their cue for this business. It not infrequently happens that when the minister comes to a full pause, after having pronounced them husband and wife, the kissing episode arrives on the scene somewhat in advance of its necessity. When young and inexperienced, I used to be obliged to pry them apart, now and then, in order to finish the service according to the rules. It makes a disconcerting moment; and inspires foolish persons, in the audience, to an unseemly levity. Indeed, you may have trouble, yourself, going through the rest of it with a sober countenance. Inform the bridegroom that when you close your book, he may kiss the bride—and not until then!

The church wedding is difficult to detail upon, so largely is this event governed by the type of building and general accommodations of the place. In the main, the same order of procession is observed as in the home wedding. It will be remembered pleasantly if your people are informed that there is no fee expected for heat, light, etc., assuming that they are—some of them—members of your church. Surely it is little enough for the church to do, on such an occasion, if it tenders the free use of its property. It is customary for the bridegroom to hand the janitor of the church a small fee to recompense him for his extra service; but if he should forget to do so, that functionary is to consider his work, on that occasion, a distinct part of his job.

As has been stated earlier, the minister's wife gets the fee. The minister should accept the wedding fee when it is tendered him. Indeed, he may go further than that, and insist upon payment, if the young fellow is mean enough to attempt an evasion of his obligation. He knows that it is the customary thing to do. It will be good discipline to see to it that he behaves like a gentleman. In twenty years, I have handed back just one wedding fee. The boy followed me out of the house, to the gate, and said: "Do you happen to have any change about you?" I replied: "Did you want some of this back?" I had not noticed the denomination of the bill he had handed me. "If you please," he answered, in some confusion, "it was ten dollars; and it is all I have. I thought I would give you about three." Having been married once myself, I figured that the whole ten dollars would not be too much with which to start on a honeymoon; so I gave it all back. But, ordinarily, the bridegroom will feel much better over the transaction if he pays.

Once, not long ago, the young fellow sought private audience with me, after the ceremony at the parsonage, and whispered that he would mail me a check in a day or two. I had not conceived a violent affection for the chap. He looked the cad, all over. So I replied—pointing to the stub on the license which was to be returned to the County Clerk—"You see that form which must be returned to the court-house before your marriage is a matter of legal record?" He nodded. "I shall mail that to the County Clerk," I said, "when I have received your check." Whereupon he said he guessed he might as well pay it now—though I suspected that his use of the word "now" made it redundant.

Occasionally, some minister reports strange events relative to the fee. The story is told of a young couple who, immediately after the evening ceremony, divested themselves of their wedding finery, and took train for New York to make close connections with an outbound steamship. Having returned from several months abroad, the bridegroom collected his evening clothes; and, in going through the pockets, gasped, hurried to the telephone, and called up the minister. He had found the twenty-dollar gold piece, carefully wrapped in tissue and enclosed in a little pasteboard box, where it had remained, undelivered, through all these many weeks. Contritely, he remarked: "Doctor Smith, I am chagrined to learn, upon my return home, that you did not receive a fee for our wedding!" "Ah, yes; but I did, Richard! It was the most interesting and unusual fee I ever received. You gave it to me, yourself." "Impossible!" said Richard. "What was it?" The minister chuckled. "It was," he replied, "a small, uncut piece of Piper Heidsieck chewing tobacco."

Preserve your relation to your wedded couples. They will be glad to be on the mailing-list of the church. When they are settled, call on them. You may properly feel that you have some claim on them, and they will appreciate your attention. Remember them on Christmas with whatever greeting you happen to be issuing. On the first anniversary of their marriage, drop them a line. Your little attentions may have more to do, than you realize, with their remembrance of the solemnity of their vows.

CHAPTER VIII

THE MINISTER'S LIBRARY

I AM not posted on the sentiment prevailing to-day among students in theological seminaries relative to ministers' libraries; but when I was in the seminary, about the time our justly celebrated twentieth century came to pass, almost everybody seemed to think it imperative that the preacher should be able to make a large showing of books on his study shelves.

In preparing to meet this forthcoming demand, many were the pitiful frugalities practised by young theologues that they might enter upon their first pastorates accompanied by an awesome array of books.

Our rivalry in the fascinating game of collecting them was intense; and because the test of the library was quantitative, rather than qualitative, we haunted the second-hand shops, rejoicing in the frequent purchase of treasures inexpensive and obsolescent. I am sure that none of our professors ever encouraged us to any such foolishness. It was a silly fad for which they were not responsible, unless it should have been a responsibility of theirs to talk to us, constructively, on the subject of the minister's library. Not realizing how ill advised was the course we took, we pursued our quest very seriously, with a zeal worthy of a more commendable enterprise

One of the heaviest losses I ever sustained was experienced during the holiday vacation of our middle year when the building which served as combination dormitory and lecture-hall burned down while we were at home for Christmas. Very few of us had been thrifty enough to carry fire insurance on our literary antiquities, so the loss was complete. It was also tragic in the extreme, considering at what mighty cost we had achieved this property. It had not occurred to us that the building and its contents might be inflammable; though we should have known that nothing on these premises could be considered a good fire risk—so dry were the ancient tomes hoarded in our rooms, to say nothing of the dryness of that which held forth in the recitation rooms on the first floor. After the conflagration, much talk was had in our church periodicals concerning the disaster, and scores of loyal alumni of the institution, learning of our bookless plight, organized a movement to replenish our devastated libraries from their own shelves. They meant it as a kindly benevolence; and I hereby register the hope that I may be forgiven the smile that is on my face as I type these reminiscent lines.

Without doubt, these good men, in their

early ministry, had been of the same mind as ourselves in regard to books, and had laid up for themselves treasures which, while subject to moth and rust, were reasonably safe from thieves who might possibly break through and steal. Having learned of our emergency, they came forward to sacrifice part of their store. We were duly grateful. I recall that I accepted my quota of these works with a thankful heart and a sober countenance. To be sure, our class did not fare quite so richly as the seniors who, very properly, I think, were given the first shot at this literary covey, but we came out of it well supplied. Most of these books were a bit too far out of date to stir one's interest to the extent of perusing them, and not quite old enough to be of value to a collector; but they were books.

With the indefatigable patience of the be-sieged spider, I set about the task of rebuilding a library which was to certify to my callers, when I had achieved a pastorate, that their young minister was evidently a person of in-dubitable scholarship. So, the gentle art of book-collecting went on, again, with feverish interest. Our efforts were redoubled because of our loss and delay. Had we ever stopped to consider the intrinsic merits of a volume before possessing it, that fact no longer weighed with us. The thing to do was to get books, no mat-ter who wrote them, or when, or how, or why.

My own collection knew no bounds as to subject-matter. It ranged all the way from a finelooking group of annual reports of the curator of the Smithsonian Institution to a rather badly battered set of Matthew Henry. This last-mentioned work I have always regarded as one of the most skilful adventures in the science of explaining the obvious and avoiding the debatable ever undertaken by mortal man. My library included a Gibbon's "Rome," minus two volumes. I contrived to get along, somehow, without the missing numbers. There were a few books reputed to be scientific in character which had been written previous to the discoveries of the past half-century. I had a book containing the addresses made at a convention of the Iowa Dairymen's Association, and another presenting a survey of the insurance companies doing business in Ohio. There were a lot of old Baedekers, and many public-school text-books.

The gifts I had received increased my wealth in such works as "Thirty Thousand Thoughts for the Thronged Theologian," "Hasty Help for the Harassed Homiletician," "The Care and Cultivation of the Lachrymal Gland," "Ready-to-Serve Anecdotes," "Saturday-Night Salvation for Shiftless Sermonizers," "New Whoops for Old Barrels," "Soft Sayings of Sobbing Sentimentalists," "Cut Gems," "Polished Jewels," "Death-Bed Remarks of Atheists," "Spectacular Conversions," and "Plenteous Pep for Pulpit Pounders." I may not be quoting these titles accurately, considerable time having elapsed since I have thought of them; but their theses might very properly have been set forth under these themes.

For fully five years I lugged this junk about with me, taking less and less pride in its possession, until it dawned upon me, one day, that the enterprise of owning and housing a library of this character was a sign of feeble-mindedness. In this, I am sure my colleagues will all agree with me; but, slightly in advance of rating me unique in this particular manifestation of imbecility, you might make a sketchy inventory of your own bookcases to determine your right to indulge in any such hilarious, homeric, cataclysmic laughter as occurs, in brackets, on the pages of the *Congressional Record*. I claim that no man who possesses in his "working library" a book he has not opened for five years is entitled to do any spoofing.

Not long after I had arrived at the momentous decision indicated above, a decrepit spring wagon backed up to our door, one morning, and about eighty per cent of my library departed therein. I sold these books by the pound; and, because old paper was not fetching much, that day, the receipts did not require me to ask for the assistance of a policeman when I went to the bank. Incidentally, you will find that whenever you have anything to sell, the market has just slumped unaccountably. It is quite different when you buy.

So much time and bother had these books cost me, through the years, that I was almost reluctant to see them go; but, once they were out of my sight, I began to rejoice in my new freedom. The old hoarding passion was gone. I was now quite at liberty to give a book away, if I wished, seeing it was of no consequence how many or how few books I displayed in my study. No longer under compulsion to build a big library, I could buy exactly the books I wanted. If I could afford to purchase five dollars' worth in the month of April, there was no reason why I should not spend the entire appropriation on a single volume, instead of distributing my budget in the interest of bulk. Henceforth and thereafter, I proposed to keep my book-shelves free of all rubbish. I have adhered to that resolution with a fair degree of fidelity. Of course one occasionally buys rubbish, thinking it to be something other; but one doesn't have to keep such things very long. Not counting reference works, I doubt if I have more than five hundred books in my possession at this moment; though if I were to have kept all the books I have bought, in the course of my ministry, they might make a very impressive showing.

It is doubtful if any man may be of much assistance to a friend when it comes to the selection of books, for the reason that there is so wide a disparity of tastes and temperaments. One man's five-foot shelf of sine qua non may prove to be stale, flat, and unprofitable to his neighbor. There are, however, certain books without which a man in our profession is seriously inconvenienced. For the benefit of you younger men in the ministry, I am going to call the roll of the books which, it seems to me, should be found in every preacher's library. Doubtless I shall omit some very important ones; but I shall not include any that is unimportant.

A good place to begin is with the Book of Books. You need one Bible that is unadorned with helps. This lies at your elbow on your study desk. It will be no extravagance if the minister possess this work in all the commonly recognized versions. Being somewhat conservative, on this subject, I do not incline toward the more chatty translations now appearing in large numbers. For the most part, these alterations of the conventional text do so little to clarify the meaning of the traditional words that it is to be doubted whether their contribution to this cause justifies the sacrifice of the historic language precious to our forebears.

It is, of course, important that religion should be revised and invoiced, from time to time, in the interest of preserving its vitality. The "old-time religion," to which many persons think we must now return, has little more to justify it than an old-time chemistry, an old-time physics, or an old-time political geography. But it is entirely possible to make adequate use of our traditional Scriptures, in their bearing upon our current moral and religious problems, without rephrasing them into the language of the market-place. In your efforts to give your people a modern interpretation of the Bible—a very good ambition—you may be tempted to read, in the pulpit, from some recent revision in which Paul is speaking after the manner of the Boys' Work Secretary at the Y. M. C. A. This is of no advantage. In a world so bewildered over the rapid and radical changes which have come to pass, in our time, it is important that we should hold fast to the actual form of certain legacies unless that form must be changed in the interest of truth. I cannot see what advantage is to be had in making the first verse of the thirteenth chapter of First Corinthians read: "Although I talk the language of humanity and the angels, and do not love, I am but making a brassy noise like a clanging cymbal."

Much fault has been found with the Catholics for conducting their religious services in Latin; nor am I disposed to consider this language properly adapted to the age and country in which we live. But whatever justification there is in it resides in the fact that these religious rites are observed in a language which, because it is no longer subject to change, possesses certain "eternal" qualities; and religion deals with matters of eternal significance. That language is positively insured against any loss which might be suffered through the introduction of transient idiom, short-lived colloquialisms, or clap-trap slang. It is not the language of barter, dicker, and trade. It is reserved for one specific use—the establishment of human-divine contacts. We Protestants cannot have that, and do not want it; but we should be on guard against tinkering too much with our traditional Scriptures. Because long patriarchal beards are not now the fashion, I doubt the wisdom of employing some modern artist to delete grandfather's whiskers from the valued portrait which hangs in the hall.

You should have a Bible containing a reliable concordance, set in readable type. A cross-reference Bible is almost a necessity. The holy books of other religions than ours are interesting to men of our calling. The Koran has a right to shelf-room in our libraries. Seeing that it is the sacred book of about one-fourth the human race, it is quite beyond the reach of our sneers. If you do not know the Upanishads, the Dhammapada, the Zend-Avesta, the Vedic Hymns, and the Life of Buddha, it's about time you went to the trouble of reading them. No religious leader need talk much about the supremacy of his faith until he is somewhat conversant with other religions than his own.

How much attention you are to pay to the Old Testament in the original is a question to be answered by yourself. If you are mentally geared to the Hebrew tongue, and enjoy working with it, one would think you would be making a mistake to neglect such research. It is doubtful if many active pastors pursue their studies in Hebrew very far past the day of graduation from the seminary. There are two excellent reasons for the study of a foreign language—mental discipline, and the practical benefits of becoming conversant with another tongue. As for the mental discipline involved in the study of Hebrew, the minister is likely to feel that he has availed himself of that in school. He has finished with it, just as he is done with Calculus. As to the practical benefits of this study, he may have reason to doubt whether his sketchy knowledge of Hebrew warrants any assurance, on his part, that his translations are even approximately correct.

My own estimate of such study is this: I am not sorry that I spent the time and went through the drudgery of learning a smattering of Hebrew in the seminary; but I am glad that it is not required of me to learn any more of it. If

you have a talent for Hebrew, keep it going.
Doubtless it repays the efforts of men who enjoy it.   If it is hard work, you can invest your
time otherwise to much better advantage.

One does not feel exactly this way about the
Greek.   In the first place, the minister is likely
to have had a good foundation of Attic Greek
in college.   Indeed, he should have had; for the
literary worker is quite at a disadvantage without it, seeing how heavily our own language is
indebted to the Greek.   In a peculiar manner,
it is a tongue that deals with power; with things
dynamic, kinetic.   The age in which we live
thinks largely in such terms.   It is to your advantage to keep up your Greek.   You will be
doing an excellent service for yourself if you
resolve to make your Greek Testament mean
as much to you as these books mean in English.

There should be at least one Bible dictionary
or encyclopædia in your library; two, if you can
afford them.   I have no notion of attempting
to offer a bibliography in this brief and casual
survey of our library essentials, but may call
your attention to certain works commonly
recognized as staples in our profession.   If you
may only have one Bible dictionary, perhaps
you should own Hastings.   If you can afford
another, the logical purchase is "The Encyclopædia Biblica."   The former is more conservative than the latter.   So soon as you are able
to have them both, get them.   If you propose

to be a workman who needeth not to be ashamed, you must have proper tools. Do your economizing somewhere else.

Doubtless you are already equipped with all the apparatus you need pertaining to dogmatics. You should be an historian. If you have never quite realized the necessity for this, let me advise you to read Doctor Shailer Mathews's "The Spiritual Interpretation of History." At no time, since the dawn of civilization, has the general public taken so large an interest in history as now. It is a significant fact that Wells's "Outline of History" is being sold in department stores. Perhaps our present bewildered state of mind, due to the rapid political, social, and economic changes in the world, accounts for the fact that so many people are eager to learn how our forebears carried on when their times were out of joint. You should be ably prepared to meet this growing demand for more light on the past. Do not rely upon any interpretation of some dramatic historical episode that you found in "The Golden Treasury of Sermonic Illustrations," or heard somewhere in a tent from the lips of an itinerant prophet. There might be somebody in your audience who, knowing the facts about that event, would instantly lose his respect for your intelligence.

The minister's chief task is to set forth a correct portrait of Jesus Christ. That being true, he should own every recognized book dealing with the Life of Christ—all of them, ancient and contemporary! And since our Christianity owes so much to the Pauline influence, there should be plenty of help, in the minister's library, to an understanding of the man of Tarsus. Not only is the preacher required to study the lives of the outstanding figures in Holy Writ, but he will find the biographies of the great a very stimulating study.

The preacher should own the best of the devotional literature. Quite a rich legacy of prayers has been traduced to us, and deserves our study. Many helpful volumes of prayers are appearing, of contemporary production, to answer the increasing demand of people who feel the need of aids to devotion. You do well to saturate yourself with the best prayers of the mystics and current religious leaders. Too little attention is being paid to this matter by many ministers. Some preachers are at their weakest when attempting to direct their congregations to God in prayer. The pulpit petition that is composed on the spot, extempore, is more often than otherwise a very wearisome and uninspiring performance. The natural inclination of the unprepared preacher, when offering a public prayer, is to assume the hortatory style. He thinks he is praying, but he is only preaching with his eyes shut. It might be remarked, in passing, that the chief defect in the average "pastoral prayer" is its extreme length, if the laymen's criticisms are to be accepted at face value. Verily, we are not heard for our much speaking. It is unimportant that we should call the roll of every trifling want. God knoweth that we have need of all these things. The prime object of prayer, after all, is not so much to make out an itemized list of our physical requirements, as to establish a human-divine relationship. Learn to lead people into a devotional mood. Study the best models. One hears occasional criticism passed upon the "book prayer" or the "read prayer," but as between a public prayer that is read impressively from a liturgy, or a rambling address to Deity, involving a recitation of current events and an invoice of the trifling tittle-tattle of the hour, one would think the choice simple enough.

Now that so much discussion is rife on the floors of great religious conclaves concerning the alleged conflict between science and religion, and the newspapers are giving front-page attention to polemic debates contingent upon this issue, the minister is expected to have some convictions anent this disputed matter. Just as the easiest way of declaring one's political faith lies in saying, "I am a Democrat," or "I am a Republican," so is it a great saving of one's time and energy to be able to announce, relative to the matter indicated above, "I am a Modernist," or "I am a Fundamentalist."

Surely you are not going to content yourself to accept the banner that somebody has thrust into your hand, and meekly follow some parade down the street, shouting a slogan that has been agreed upon as best appealing to the untutored imagination of the mass! You can afford to do some thinking, on your own account. If you do not relish the idea of being herded into one or the other of these two corrals, there is no reason why you should submit to such treatment. If you want to vote a scratched ballot, that is your right.

Humanity has had occasion to revise the terms of its religious beliefs, many times; and it appears that our generation has been asked to undertake this task again. Considerable anxiety is being displayed by the conservatives —and not without some warrant—lest, in this reappraisal of religion to make it consonant with modern thought, the fundamentals may become obscured. This is a very real apprehension. In a time like this, there is always a danger of "throwing the baby out with the bath."

Being somewhat weary of that word "fundamentals," which has taken on the aspect of a cultus, let me speak of these imperatives of religion as "the elements." I think we are all agreed that the elements of Christ's teaching may be summarized under three general heads —faith, love, and service. If we emphasize these principles, and succeed in committing our congregations to them, I do not fear that we will find ourselves losing the respect of scientific men. They, themselves, in the course of conferring larger benefits upon our social order through the application of research in the fields of surgery, histology, chemistry, and other prophylactic and remedial activities, are putting these principles to work—the Christ principles of faith, love, and service. Neither will we find ourselves sustaining awkward relationships with students of "the humanities," if we can show them that their cause is also ours. But to back up, stolidly, against the ivied gothic of traditional "churchianity," and defend its dogmatism declared in days remote, on another continent, against the invasion of contemporaneous thought concerning life, is to deal a blow at the cause we had hoped to serve.

This insistent call on the part of so many people, to-day, for a solution of our problems of religious belief by a return to a more vigorous insistence upon the effete adiaphora of the ancient creeds and confessions is a serious disclosure of unwillingness or inability to measure up to the demands put upon our generation. Instead of making the adventure of seeing this matter through to a satisfactory solution, many are disposed to choose the easy way, and say: "Let us turn back!" Having come to the crossroad, and being somewhat undecided which way to turn, we are advised to retrace our steps in the direction from whence we have come.

No; the problem will not be solved by our denial of what latter-day chemistry and physics have made clear, or in our sneering at the discoveries of archæologists, ethnologists, paleontologists, and anthropologists. Neither is it permitted us to sink back, with a weary sigh, and remark yawningly: "Oh, well, these things haven't anything to do with religion, after all!" Yes—but they have! At the present hour, they have almost everything to do with religion! An attitude of serene indifference to this problem may satisfy your layman of seventy-plus, who may have formed his mental habits more than a half-century ago; but you now have a new generation on your hands, for whom light has been broken into many more colors than used to be refracted through a prism!

If you are seriously in earnest about wanting to keep abreast of the modern thinking on these disputed subjects, secure the books written by men recognized as experts in these respective fields. Read the works of men who are interested in the study of evolution, for example, not as it affects or is affected by religion, but who treat of it in the dispassionate mood of the truth-seeker who is not trying to make out a good case for some pet theory. If you would inform yourself concerning this matter, it is much better that you should secure your data from people who are not out to demonstrate any given theological hypothesis—either liberal or conservative.

Whatever conclusions you arrive at, be honest. Be intellectually moral. I have heard men denouncing evolution (which they so commonly refer to, these days, as "Darwinism"— albeit Charles Darwin is related to the present-day theory of evolution very much as Robert Fulton is related to modern steam-navigation). When queried as to the extent of their familiarity with Darwin's writings, they not only admit but boast that they have not yet contaminated their minds—they are proud to state —with any such untenable trash. This, I should say, is a very unfortunate state of mind for any man to be in who is looked upon as a moral leader.

Chemistry is brimful of striking illustrations for pulpit use. Medicine and surgery provide apt suggestions, too. Books are to be had, stating in non-technical terms, some of the most interesting developments in these fields. The doctor is always appreciative when you refer to the advancement in his profession; provided you speak with knowledge. Perhaps it will please you to own a large number of the little books now appearing which explain, simply, so many of life's activities. Take "Navigation" as a sample. This little primer will help you to the right nautical phrase, if you are in doubt.

Even so far away from the sea as Kansas, your remark in Wichita that the captain had thrown the hawsers back upon the pier, drawn in the gangway, and boxed the compass, prefatory to setting forth upon his long voyage, would probably fetch a grin to the countenance of some descendant of a maritime family. Check all your illustrations for accuracy. Not many will bring you to book for your mistakes in theology; but they will be inclined to discount the whole of your knowledge if they find it inaccurate in matters of technical detail with which they are familiar. Build into your library all the aids you can find to insure against these blunders.

Read essays—ancient and modern. Read plays. Keep informed about contemporary verse; it may be assumed that you have the standard classics. Provide yourself with an abundance of nature studies. The habits of ants, bees, wasps, and spiders—how wealthy we have become in literature on this subject.

Every library possessed by one engaged in literary composition should include the standard apparatus of the craft; to wit, one good desk dictionary, a more pretentious dictionary to fall back upon when the little one has reached the end of its tether, a manual of style, a book of synonyms, and a few volumes of stock citations from classic poems, plays, essays, and orations, from which you may quickly verify the verbal accuracy of some quotation you wish to make, but only half remember. You should have a good general encyclopædia, and make diligent use of it. When you have an unclaimed half-hour on your hands, and are scouting for a new line of thought, take down a volume of the encyclopædia and leaf it through —not searching for anything in particular, but on a general tour of discovery.

You should own the best sermons of the great preachers; but you are not to read any one of these sermons while you happen to be at work on the specific theme of which it treats. A great deal of unintentional and perhaps unconscious plagiarism may be committed by having the sermon of some other man too fresh in your mind while wrestling with the same thesis.

There should be a good reading-lamp at the head of your bed; and, every night, you should have a book at hand with which to bring the day to a delightful close. My own choice, for such reading, is the travel book. The day's work is done. I am stealing no time from anybody if I read exactly what pleases my own fancy, now, for I am supposed to be asleep. Any oculist will tell you that it is a vicious habit to read in bed. Maybe so. But the travel book is the thing, unquestionably.

CHAPTER IX

THE MINISTER'S MAIL

TWO dips of a pen in a bottle of ink are good for fifty words, within which limits a great deal may be said. Two cents suffice to carry this message to its destination. So if the minister has just learned that the Parkers have achieved a new grandson, the pleasure of going on record with his full approval of the movement is easy and inexpensive. With low-test gasolene priced at twenty-six cents per gallon, and every hour of the preacher's daylight as precious as the great auk is rare, it really isn't necessary that he should call upon the Parkers to felicitate them upon the advent of their grandchild in a neighboring State. Indeed, the Parkers are not expecting any notice to be taken by him of this event which has brought them so much joy. If he recognizes the matter, at all, his courtesy is a bit of bonus added to their happiness. He can attend to this in five minutes or less, lick a stamp, mail the note, and the deed is performed. The Parkers rejoice in the communication, read it to the neighbors, and remail it to Helen, who triumphantly shows it to the baby.

The Strattons, having resolved to spend the summer in Europe, are delighted to have a letter from the minister in which he expresses his pleasure over this really wonderful experience so soon to be theirs; for this is the first trip abroad, and the prospect of it has eclipsed every other fact in the Strattons' lives. To show their appreciation, they send him post-cards from every port of call, and are almost overcome with affection for him when they find a letter from him waiting for them at the American Express office in Geneva. It doesn't have to be a long letter; the shorter the better, indeed, for they are busy folk, these days, rushing about from tomb to shrine, trying to see it all. His total investment in the Strattons, to date, has cost about ten cents, counting postage and stationery, plus fifteen minutes of his time; and now the Strattons are friends of his for life. One can't have things so desirable as the Strattons' lasting affection for less cost.

Johnnie Thompson's name has appeared in the evening paper topping a list of the high-school seniors who made all A's. Johnnie deserves congratulation from the minister of his church. A few lines certifying that the minister is proud to have such fine, upstanding chaps in his congregation will insure him a fresh grip on Johnnie's heart; and Johnnie's father and mother will bear up under it, too, with great fortitude. Gladys Williams is reported to be leaving, presently, for Philadelphia, to study nursing. A personal call is not demanded here;

but a note of approval and warm commendation will help her mightily through those first weeks of loneliness and the drudgery which the novice in her profession experiences.

Every morning, immediately after breakfast, the shepherd of the flock can invest a half-hour very profitably by writing a half-dozen such letters as these. They need not be extended letters. After one has completed the first page of such a message, it is probable that whatever one adds, thereafter, will amount to subtraction. A few words are ample to convey the idea that the shepherd is genuinely concerned over the welfare of his flock. If he keeps his eyes open and his ears to the ground, he will be learning, every day, of the big and little things his parishioners are doing in the general interest of the public weal. These specific forms of service should be recognized. The Youngs have donated some radium to the Providence hospital. They don't have to be members of his church to get a letter from him in which he tells them that they are of the Brotherhood of the Burning Heart. Not only do they richly deserve commendation, from his quarter, but it encourages them to further investments of their means in the cause of altruism.

It is a great thing to keep in mind certain birthdays, especially of the aged and infirm; and at least the first anniversary of a serious bereavement. "He remembered!" they remark, as the note is passed from hand to hand on the day when the whole tragedy surges over them again, fresh as if it had happened yesterday. Last year's date-book should lie on the minister's desk, ready to provide him with the data necessary to the proper timing of these letters. It is frequently the case that the minister can make his personal services and friendship more valuable to the young men and women of his parish who are away at college than when they were at home. Especially at examination time are they in the market for notes of encouragement, with just a touch of serious admonition to the effect that Plunkville expects every man to do his duty.

It may be entirely superfluous to add that such letters as are suggested above should be pen-written. Of course it is easier to dictate them to a stenographer, or type them oneself; but they are never quite so convincing when done through a third party, or on a machine. The business of writing with a pen is irksome, no doubt; but it is very excellent discipline. The machine is almost too fluent for the operator's good. Many a preacher would develop a finer and more forceful rhetorical style by returning to the laborious process of pen-writing, occasionally. It is possible for a man of our profession to achieve such proficiency with the typewriting machine that he records his ideas faster than they accrue.

Chiefly is this admonition presented to the ministerial brother who possesses what has come to be known among our craft as "the fatal gift of letter-writing." The unfortunate letter-writer can do himself a greater disservice, in a briefer length of time, with a machine than a pen. He is peevish about something, we will suppose, and sits down at his typewriter to splutter his indignation. The thing is capable of recording his wrath as rapidly as he emits it. Remarks which he would never think of making with a pen exude from him at this moment. Many a preacher has done himself out of his pastorate and his most substantial friends by way of an imprudent letter, written in haste and anger. Sometimes it has been a fourteen-page epistle to Deacon Strong, phrased "in all candor," relative to some sensitive situation probably involving matters of administration. Not infrequently it is a whimpering document addressed to some disaffected member of the church in the town whose dust he has but recently shaken from his feet—a general inventory of the ills from which he has flown to make adventure with others which, at this date, he knows not of. Not content with having foozled his job so badly that he left the church in a state of disruption, he desires to make the disaster complete by cuddling what little is left to him, in that place, of friendship nurtured in a sense of grievance.

That which is written in ink cannot hope to possess the lasting qualities of remarks done into the wall with a mallet and chisel; but it is sufficiently enduring to survive for a long time after their author has repented of his hasty imprudence; and he who commits his ill humor to paper should reflect, while sealing the envelope, that so soon as he pushes this thing into the mail-box, the deed is done. Many a man, in a testy mood, impulsively writes scathing letters to people with whom he happens to find himself in disagreement, thereby discrediting himself in the opinion of men who suspect that he might not possess either the courage or audacity to say these things, were they met face to face.

Every preacher, whose pulpit and platform work is carried on with a degree of fearlessness, can expect to be a target for much caustic criticism hurled at him through the mail. Some of these letters are anonymous, and many more of them are practically anonymous, so little do the signatures matter. If he is thin-skinned, these yips and snarls of his ungracious critics are likely to worry him. No matter how nonchalant he may seem to be in his attitude toward such unsolicited correspondence, letters of this sort always leave a bad taste in his mouth. His natural inclination may prompt him to reply, at once, with the biggest shot he has in his locker. He will do well to remember that if he is too sensitive to stand up under unfair and ungentlemanly attacks made upon him because of his public utterances, he has no business to indulge himself in any freedom of speech. Merely because the other fellow has lost his temper, and has called him hard names, does not excuse the preacher for climbing down to wallow in the mud with his opponent.

You younger men of the profession must be constantly on guard against falling victim to the strange delusion which obsesses many of our own calling who apparently feel privileged to ransack the whole vocabulary of execration to find terms mean enough to launch at persons of other opinions than their own. In the course of twenty years in the ministry, I have had quite a large number of letters written to me, in critical mood. Many of them have been almost beyond endurance and beneath contempt. The very smallest and meanest of them have been received from preachers who chose this singular manner of convincing me how much more holy and worthy was their interpretation of religion than my own. I think it may be put down as a general rule that a man does himself a bad turn when he writes anything that he knows he wouldn't have the inclination or the brass to say to his correspondent were they facing each other, astraddle of a log, ten miles from camp. It doesn't take much courage to be heroic and sassy by mail or over the telephone. A very small man can scribble some very large words.

All this is suggested by the thought that every scrap of mail that goes out of the preacher's office should be dignified, temperate, and gracious, no matter what may be the provocation to requite the ungenerous in the coin with which they appear to be most familiar. You will get all sorts of communications from all sorts of people. Most of it is pleasant; some of it is infuriating. You will receive badly misspelled advices from people you didn't know were in existence. One nice old lady wrote to me, once, after hearing an address of mine, that she doubted if I had ever saved any "soals." Of course the raw insolence of this makes a heavy drain upon one's patience. You will discover that the bulk of the letters you receive from people who are disposed to put you on the grill are conceived in ignorance and brought forth in illiteracy. That must not mislead you into the belief that all of the intelligentsia are on your side, and all the roughnecks and boneheads are of the opposition. It means only that the majority of the people who hastily grab up a pen to indite billingsgate, on any subject, are not likely to give evidence of much refinement of manner or magnanimity of mind.

The gentle art of correspondence has slumped. Most men are too busy, or think they are—which comes to the same thing—to put themselves on paper in a leisurely, gracious, contemplative mood.   But there are a few who are not yet so completely stampeded and panic-driven by their multitudinous duties that they have no time or opportunity for an occasional exchange of the written word.   One of the most enjoyable of the few recreations I indulge in is the correspondence I maintain with a small group of men whose time appears to have been sufficiently well organized that they can afford to give me a half-hour of it, now and then. When I write to these people, I put my best foot foremost.   I am inclined to believe that they are somewhat meticulous in the choice of their language when they write to me; and I must show my appreciation by doing my very best for them.   They tell me about the new books they are reading.   Sometimes those comments are ever so much better than the books, as I discover later.   They give me the benefit of their private thinking on the live issues of the day.   Not infrequently they tell me a funny story.   It is a delight to get such letters.   But, as usual, it is even more blessed to give than to receive.   The painstaking composition of one's outgoing mail, addressed to the members of this fraternity, is excellent exercise.   The homilist really needs some avocation of this sort to keep his style fresh and vigorous.   Most of us take ourselves all too seriously.

Now, to make a delight of correspondence,

one should be supplied with the proper tools. First, there is the paper. Perhaps not everybody feels the same way about this; but, to me, a letter is always so much more interesting if it is written on good paper. It is a compliment to have a letter that represents at least a slight investment on the part of the writer. To receive a communication written on cheap note-paper hastily ripped out of a tablet, all ragged at the top, makes one think poorly of oneself. If old Polonius will permit a liberty to be taken with his celebrated advice to his son, I would suggest to the youth of our profession: "Costly thy paper as thy purse can buy." If an engraved letter-head is an extravagance for you, be sure that it is at least a good job of printing. Don't feel necessitated to include, in this printed matter, the hours of the stated meetings held in your church, or any pious maxims wrought in your homiletic laboratory. It is barely possible that you may have earned some degrees; perhaps other dignities have been conferred upon you by way of recognition of good service. But your stationery will look so much neater if uncluttered with these ornaments.

This business of selecting a style of stationery and letter-head should be undertaken with much care; for you don't want to change your policy every time you find yourself out of paper. If it means something for a business house to adopt a style of stationery, bearing the name of the firm in a device which persists through the years, it means quite as much for you to pursue the same policy. Don't tinker with your name. It is bad business to sign yourself variously—A. B. Jones, Arthur B. Jones, A. Browning Jones, Arthur Browning Jones, etc. Resolve early what kind of a Jones you propose to be, and stick to it through thick and thin.

Perhaps it is not necessary to say that we need not feel under compulsion to use the old stock phrases which make so much business correspondence tiresome and lifeless. It is silly to write: "Your favor of the tenth instant is at hand and contents noted and in reply would say—" whatever it is that you would say. It's dull enough to get stuff like this that has been milled through the shop of some third assistant to the vice-department-head in a business concern; but when it comes from offices handling the character of business that we do, it is inexcusable. Put a bit of sparkle and spontaneity into your letters. Be direct and businesslike; but avoid the old stereotyped phrases.

Keep a watchful eye out for the brother who addresses you "My Christian Friend" and subscribes himself "Yours in Jesus' Name." This will probably turn out to be an invitation to purchase a few shares of oil stock to protect a very fine lease that is located in the imagination of somebody who holds forth from the fifty-first floor of a tall building on Manhattan Island. Or, if it isn't that, you may discover it to be an appeal from some sect like "The Holy and Triumphant Saints of God" who wish you to take up a collection to aid them in putting a new roof on their place of worship in Zanzibar.

Be wary of the ex-minister who signs himself "Rev." So-and-so—and has some beautiful real estate to dispose of, at a sacrifice, among his ministerial brethren. He will tell you that he wants to do you good; and so he will, if you give him a chance. Your mail-box will always be gorged with alluring offers of stocks which are to make you wealthy. You can put it down as a safe proposition that any stock which is required to be peddled by mail, or otherwise, among the members of our profession—traditionally poor and without a financial margin—is fraudulent. And while on this subject of investments—for quite a large percentage of the preacher's incoming mail is publicity matter from fake brokerage houses—you ought to know that when any man wants to sell you stocks on ridiculously small instalments, he is peddling something that has already been milked dry at headquarters. Is it reasonable to suppose that any concern would go to the bother of hawking its certificates among the preachers, to be paid for in little dribs, if the

stuff was worth having? Stocks which have
any apparent future are all gobbled up by the
people who have first access to them. Moreover, the agent knows this full well; and when
he approaches you with his wild tale about
prompt and easy riches for you by this process,
you are justified in talking to him in precisely
the same tone you would probably employ were
he to say: "Reverend Easymark, I consider you
an imbecile."

We were talking about tools. You cannot do
all of your writing with a pen. The bulk of
your correspondence will be done with a machine. You can afford to have a good typewriter. It is to be doubted if you can afford to
have a poor one. You may have discovered,
ere this, that it is easier to go back over a misspelled word and stamp it out with a string of
xxxx's, than to erase the blunder. You have
learned that when in doubt whether the word
is spelled with an "ei" or an "ie," it is quite
simple to type it both ways, and let the reader
take his choice. Perhaps you have sometimes
gone back to an *s*, and pounded a *z* on top of it
in cases where there was some reason to doubt
which of these letters the occasion demanded.
Some day you will send a sloppily written thing
like that to the one man who may have it all
to say whether or not you get the chance to
improve your fortunes; and he will remark:
"I don't like the way his mind works!" Buy

a fresh ribbon for your machine frequently. See that the carriage gives you a left margin without any short lines. Adopt an office style, and adhere to it. If you resolve to indent every paragraph five spaces, don't alter the resolution. Standardize your processes of correspondence, so that when anybody who knows you picks up a letter of yours, he can identify it. This method gives people the impression that you are orderly of mind and steady of purpose. You owe it to yourself to create and conserve that impression.

It is not necessary to file all the letters one receives. Seventy-five per cent of them, probably, have no future use, and are better off in the waste-basket so soon as they have received attention. But it is well to retain—for perusal on drab days—the little notes you get, from time to time, telling you how wonderfully you have helped somebody. It makes a fine antidote to take for some of the nasty medicine that is sure to come to you if you say anything at all that is worth saying in your pulpit. I have sorted out a few really nice letters and pasted them in a book. When I shall have come into my sear and yellow, I propose to comfort myself, occasionally, with them; and let them remind me that it was all worth doing, if for no better reason than to achieve these delightful rewards.

CHAPTER X

SERMON-MAKING

NO small part of the minister's everyday life is occupied with the preparation of sermons. I hesitate to invade this field, because I make no pretense at being a skilled homiletician, and this book is not a homiletic treatise. But the fact remains that one cannot speak of the duties of our profession without considering this function which is, beyond question, the most important service we render.

The minister who permits his multifarious civic and social obligations to minify his usefulness as a preacher will discover that while he may be regarded as a very fine fellow and an efficient errand-boy for two dozen philanthropic organizations, more or less actively engaged in social service, his ability as a religious leader and spiritual adviser is questionable, even in the minds of his most ardent admirers.

Doubtless most of the dull preaching that one hears so much about, these days, is due, largely, to the lack of a long-term programme of sermonizing. It is to be suspected that too many preachers do not know, with certainty,

what their next Sunday's sermons are to be
about until Thursday morning, when, they are
reminded, it is time to send the topics to the
papers. Any man who is ambitious to become
a really useful and successful preacher should
be warned that this is not a promising way to
proceed. He should know, in the first week
of March, what his morning sermon is to treat
of on the first Sunday of May, assuming the
morning service to be the chief event in his
church.

Fortunately, the seasons of the church year,
and certain outstanding commemorative events
nationally observed, serve as general guides to
the planning of many if not most of the sermons
in American pulpits. So rapidly have these
"special days" found their way into the minister's calendar, in recent years, that a mild
protest is being raised against the further en-
croachment upon his homiletic options. If the
various "causes" had their way, we could easily
assign every Sunday of the year to a discussion
of the philanthropies undertaken by certain
zealous groups of humanitarians. We are entirely justified in giving time and attention to
the most widely recognized, and established, of
these movements; but the preacher who heeds
every summons to advocate a cause soon finds
himself with a very restless and half-starved
flock on his hands. It seems hardly necessary
to spend a Sunday morning in celebration of

"Be-kind-to-animals Day." If the Christianity taught in that place is functioning properly, it may be assumed that the people who belong to the institution are endeavoring to be
as decent as possible to the animals, all the
year round.

It may be of interest to make a brief survey
of the possibilities offered by the more important
festivals, ecclesiastical and secular. Let us ar-
bitrarily begin with the opening of the church's
activities in the late summer. We will suppose
that the minister has been away on his vacation. He should have a vacation. Only an
extraordinary minister can do as much work
in twelve months as he can do in eleven. An
occasional objection is raised to the minister's
month off, on the ground that the Devil never
takes a vacation. Unless it is presumed that
the minister should try, so far as possible, to
model his programme after that of the hypothetical person just mentioned, that objection
points no moral.

Your vacation should be spent elsewhere than
within the bounds of your own parish. Now
and then, a minister announces that he is not
going away, this summer. He will do his rest-
ing at home. It cannot be done; and nobody
ever tries it more than once. Merely to be
excused from one's pulpit obligations for a
month means very little. The pastoral responsibility does not ease up, for a moment,

and that is, after all, the heavy part of the minister's load. Go as far away as your resources will permit, preferably out in the open where nature is on display in the rough, and living conditions are different from those which obtain at home.

If you are quite in love with your profession, you may find that, after an idle week, you are thinking considerably about your programme for the coming autumn. Without meaning to encourage you to sacrifice a single minute to your work that really should be spent in play —for the sake of your vigor and physical fitness —I should suppose that you will arrive home with a fairly definite plan for your pulpit work over a period of two months, perhaps.

The first Sunday of September, if you are back from your vacation, then, is booked for you; so you need have no worriment about that. It is Labor Sunday. Do not expect things to start off with a bang, that day; for Monday is a holiday, and many people have decided to take these days off for a brief trip, somewhere. They can start early Saturday afternoon, and stay away until Tuesday morning, when school begins. Your congregation will be small and disspiriting. Because I am a believer in starting off the fall season in the church with every yard of canvas to the breeze, I time my vacation so that I am not yet returned on Labor Sunday. Experience has taught me that it requires more effort to generate a given amount of momentum, in the church, by observing Labor Sunday than omitting it.

If you are on hand, Labor Sunday, pull through the best way you can, censuring no one for your small audience and feeble beginning. Many of these absentees are taking the only days off that are permitted to them. Do not scold.

The schools having opened, there is a good reason for your preaching, on the following Sunday, concerning the interrelated obligations of parents, teachers, and scholars. There will be some new teachers in town. As strangers, they may welcome a mailed announcement stating your theme. If it pleases you to shape your discourse so that you are speaking directly to the teachers, you can make use of this device to tell the congregation something about the fineness and importance of the service the teacher renders the State. Should you announce that you will speak on "Beyond the Curriculum," you will have a chance to talk to the teachers of their opportunity to create ideals, and influence budding thought, quite aside from the mere drudgery of imparting information on "the three r's." After you have done this, you may have reason to believe that it was one of the most valuable and effective services of the year.

On the next Sunday, you may find it convenient to observe what some church schools call "Rally Day," or, still better, "Recognition Day"—when the necessity of systematic religious education is brought attractively to the attention of your people, and the school is conducted in a manner that draws respectful attention. This leaves only one more Sunday in September to plan for. This will afford you an opportunity to preach one of those monumental sermons that you blocked out while roaming through the woods.

I find it of much advantage to preach "series" sermons, generally about four to the group. When one announces a longer series than that, both the preacher and the congregation are likely to be tired of it before it is done. Moreover, you will find it difficult to secure more than four consecutive Sundays without missing some important church festival or national event worthy of observance. Sometimes you can so arrange a series of sermons that the one which happens to occur on a festival day may be used in conjunction with that issue; for example: we will suppose that you have announced a series for October on "Spiritual Portraits." In your advance publicity—for of course you will want to prepare and mail to each household of your membership, and the "prospectives," a neatly printed four-page folder, setting forth the themes to be treated, and your reasons for addressing yourself to this particular cause at

this time—you could say that we, who are alleged to be progressive in our theology, are in
the habit of referring to the narratives in
Genesis as "the folk-lore of the early Hebrews"
—not to be considered as actual photographs
of historical events, but rather as "spiritual
portraits" of the moral problems which men
have always encountered everywhere. Too frequently, having commented feelingly upon the
richness and beauty of these "spiritual portraits," we go on about our other business without pausing to explain to our people exactly
wherein that same' richness and beauty resides. So you can do it now in this series.
Obviously, your first sermon of the group will
be on "The Creation." Be honest, as a student, in dealing with the Adam legend, but be
sure you find the "portrait."

You will discover that this is good pulpit
business in these times of unusual interest in
the theory of evolution. If you are tactful,
sympathetic, and mindful of your terms, you
should be able to present an interpretation of
modern thought on this subject, almost anywhere, without having to send in a riot call to
the police. It is better to keep away from that
word "evolution." There are a half-dozen ac-
ceptable synonyms. You may be able to convince some people that your ideas are every
way worthy of respect when you talk about
"racial development." Were you to have said

"evolution," they might have balked. "Natural progression"—that is a good phrase, and comes to the same thing. Just now, the word "evolution" is like a red rag to a bull, especially in the opinion of people who know little or nothing about it. Doubtless this is why the bull is afraid of the red rag; if he knew what it was, he would have no fear of it.

The second sermon of the October series may treat of "The Deluge." There is a great story here. You can contrast the redemption of a single household in a wooden boat with the redemption of the whole social order on a wooden cross. If you have the nerve, you might add that it was not a cross, either, that burned with the flames of sectarian hatred, but adrip with sacrificial blood! The third sermon should consider the pioneering patriarchs in the Promised Land. "The Quest" would be a good title for it. You will be doing this on the Sunday nearest to the commemoration of the discovery of America; and if you cannot make Abraham and Columbus come to speaking terms with each other, in this sermon, your imagination needs a massage. They went out—both of them—not knowing whither they went, but plainly declaring that they sought a country. The last sermon of the group might deal with "The Exodus." He is not much of a preacher who cannot make that story stand up and breathe in these times of utter bewilderment on the part of men and nations, seeking "a road out" of their present predicaments.

If your congregation seems to relish this idea of a consecutive chronological study of the Old Testament, and large audiences have been secured, keep up steam and go on while the going is good. Announce another series for November. Call it "Ancient Hebrew Kings"—or the equivalent of that. The public is temporarily interested in the ancient kings. So long as the people are talking about the tomb of Tutankh-Amen, you may be assured of a hearing if you talk about his contemporaries. In this group of four sermons tell the stories of Saul, David, Solomon, and Rehoboam.

You should not forget to plan well in advance for your Thanksgiving Day service. It is not enough to celebrate that occasion on the Sunday previous to this unique American festival, or content yourself with a mid-week Thanksgiving talk on Wednesday evening. Thanksgiving should be observed on Thursday. Make use of this event. It is the only "all-American" religious festival on the calendar. All the people are agreed about Thanksgiving. It is insured against any sectarian prejudices. The churches are urged, by a presidential decree, to observe the day. It has become customary, in many places, for a "union service" to be planned, in which (theoretically, but not practically) a group of churches, geographically related, pool their interests. These "union" meetings are rarely worth the bother, which is a scant tribute to them since nobody goes to much bother to make them successful. Because it is a "union service," no one feels any keen responsibility for it, and it is usually a fizzle. It is held in the Presbyterian church, the Methodist minister is preaching the sermon, and the Baptist choir is furnishing the music. Because he is not in charge of the affair, the Presbyterian minister thinks he has done his bit by instructing the janitor to have the church unlocked and heated. Because it is not his church that the service is held in, the Methodist preacher considers his duty limited to the address he has promised to deliver. The Baptist choir leader confers with nobody, hoping to receive full instructions when he arrives at the church. A little handful of people—less than three hundred, perhaps—come out to the service. Three hundred people, in an auditorium capable of taking care of eight hundred people, have a sense of being associated with a lost cause, whether that occurs on Thanksgiving Day or any other day. An insignificant cash collection is taken, to be turned over to the local charities; and the dismal enterprise is over for another year. Announce your own Thanksgiving Day service. In all of your publicity matter, beginning in early November, keep this coming event before the attention of your people. Your choir should have anthems in rehearsal in anticipation of this day, so long as six weeks before it occurs. If you wish, you may pack your church on Thanksgiving morning. It's all up to you.

The public begins to think about Christmas quite early in the season. The sooner you begin to capitalize this Christmas concept, the better off you are. Have your December sermons built around the idea, and make an attractive series of them. The merchants will be saying: "Do your Christmas shopping early, before the stock is all picked over!" Be as good a psychologist, and induce a Christmas state of mind before your people are being hammered with it on every side commercially. It is well to have your Christmas series of sermons all ready to announce on Thanksgiving Day.

These December sermons can be made a great delight. Some time try a series on "What Christmas Has Brought to Civilization." In four sermons, consider Christ as an economist, a sociologist, a statesman, and a theologian. You will not wish to phrase them so academically as that; but these attributes of the Master would provide you with your thesis. A fruitful group of December sermons is a study of "Historic Christmas-Tides." The specific themes of the first three might be "Christmas in the Fourth Century," "Christmas with the Crusaders," and "Christmas with the Pilgrims."

The group would arrive at a satisfactory climax with "Christmas in 1924." The people learn something about church history, from these sermons, which is good for them. More and more I am coming to believe that we cannot place too much emphasis upon that legacy of faith and sacrifice bequeathed to us from a mighty past. It means a very great deal to be in and of an institution that has the right to apostrophize "the glorious company of the apostles, the goodly fellowship of the prophets, the noble army of martyrs, and the holy church throughout all the world." In this opportunistic day of ours, and in this rapidly growing country, where our most venerable works seem to reek of fresh paint, green lumber, and hot rivets, it is not a bad idea to get out the ancient treasures, once in a while, and let the people see the portraits of our spiritual ancestry.

On the Sunday preceding the New Year, your case is made for you. Perhaps you will be glad to spend the month of January on independent sermons of an evangelistic nature. Once in a long time, it is a good idea to omit the announcement of subjects for a few Sundays. There will be an element of surprise in this plan. Be on guard that you do not surprise the congregation by being unprepared. The fact that you did not publicly announce your themes in advance is not to mean that you, yourself, were unaware what would be the motion before the house.

February brings Lincoln and Washington into focus. If you are in a place where you may do so without risk of more damage than good, you might remember that Darwin and Lincoln, who made adventures in the cause of liberty, by different routes, were born on the same day. Lent will begin presently. If you are the minister of a church that is accustomed to the observance of Lent, your course is more or less definitely prescribed. If your church has paid no attention to Lent, do your people the good service of proving its value to them. An excellent way to induce a Lenten mood is through a group of three sermons on "The Temptations." That is what Lent is about, anyway. This study of the temptations is practically inexhaustible. Not only are these three episodes brimming with moral and spiritual precepts, but they are intensely practical. Can you think of anything more immediately concerned with the problems of our day than the economic considerations involved in the Master's struggle over the relative importance of his life-work and his appetite? Whether or not man does live "by bread alone" is a vital question. Should it not be of interest and value to our present crop of Americans to hear the Master's decision on the problem whether it is better to gamble with Providence and attempt to take a short cut to fame and influence, or make haste slowly? "Thou shalt not put the Lord thy God to a test!" is a live issue. And how the nations of the world are to be won by the Prince of Peace—does that not concern us, tremendously, to-day?

Sunday-evening sermons, through the period of early spring, should accommodate themselves to the fact that people are tired of winter, and eager to emerge from their cramped quarters. They want to travel. They are afflicted with wanderlust. If you ever travelled abroad, tell them about it now. Give them a group of sermons on Paul's missionary journeys.

Be sure to celebrate Holy Week effectively. Do not be satisfied with a little "prayer-meeting group" in a corner of the Sunday-school assembly-room, on the nights of that week. Hold your service in the church auditorium, with full choir on duty, and the preacher ably prepared. If at all practicable, have your Good Friday service in the afternoon at three. There is no service of the whole year, in my church, that is quite so impressive as this, or better attended. It is a great opportunity. You must not miss it.

We have a tradition, in our profession, to the effect that there is a general "let down" after Easter. The minister has had a long, hard run, gathering in intensity as he reaches the Day of Resurrection, and he is very tired. Easter used up the last of his neural resources. It began with the sunrise meeting, out on a hilltop, perhaps. (If you have not tried this, make the experiment. You may be amazed to see the large number of people who will welcome it, and attend it.) Easter was full of events in which the minister was required to be at his best. He is thoroughly fagged. Perhaps he should book an exchange of pulpits, with a neighbor, on the following Sunday.

Make the most of the budding spring. People are anxious to see it arrive. Phrase your topics to intrigue the imagination that longs for the return of flowers and sunshine. Life is full of renewals—renewals of hope, courage, industry, and idealism. There's a series of sermons for you.

Mother's Day is good for a crowd, no matter what you do. We must be careful to keep this festival from becoming a mere matter of slushy sentiment. There is a chance, here, to do some real constructive work on "The Reappraisement of Womanhood." Now that the patient, resigned mother of the old days, who sat by the window, knitting stockings for her grandchildren, has been succeeded by a new type of mother, who plays tennis, drives her own car, and pursues a social programme that would have brought her own mother, at that age, to a not very honorable grave—we must reshape our advices on the subject of motherhood. The question is not, whether the modern mother is better or worse than her predecessor. The problem resides in the fact that she is different!

June brings Commencement, Children's Day, and an opportunity to specialize on a group of sermons to adolescents. Their parents will come, too, if you have anything worth while for the youngsters. You cannot preach "heavy" sermons in June, anyway. The weather is not conducive to the success of inductive logic; so, if you are obliged to preach very simply, why not address yourself specifically to the children? Prepare a patriotic sermon for the Sunday preceding the Fourth of July. Don't begin to slip, about the third Sunday of the month that was named for Uncle Julius, and claw around in the barrel for some of your mildewed homiletic preserves. You will think better of yourself, and have a finer time on your vacation, if you keep the thing going—one hundred per cent right—to the very last hour of the last day before you knock off for your well-earned leave.

I suppose you have a right to expect that there will be some talk, in this chapter, about the actual business of sermon construction. As I remarked earlier, I do not pose as an authority on this subject, and if you are hoping that I will tell you something about the mechanical engineering feat of building a sermon so that the introduction will consume one-ninth of the time given to the argument, and the conclusion one-eleventh, you are in for a disappointment. I never yet attempted to build a sermon with my watch in one hand and a yardstick in the other. If you wish information on that matter, are these things not written in the chronicles of divers and sundry sermon-smiths?

Such advice as I may offer is general. First: keep yourself in a "homiletic mood." This state of mind is not unlike that of the news-gatherer on the local staff of the daily paper. Everything he sees is potential news. He puts every sight and sound through his reportorial laboratory to test it for its news value. You must be in a homiletic mood, seven days of the week, waking and sleeping. When the plumber comes to your house, and you know he is in the basement, gouging around in the gloom, among the water-pipes, go down and get acquainted with him. Make him talk; and, when you have him going, listen to what he says. Talk to the taxi-driver. Visit the fire-engine house. Make friends with policemen. Attend the municipal court occasionally. Go to the jail. Spend an afternoon at the County Infirmary. Find out how they got there. Go down to the foundry, about four o'clock in the afternoon, and watch them pour. Talk to the man who runs the dog-store. Spend an hour with the man who supervises the collection of the city waste. Ask the man who sells magazines about the demand in his business. After he has told you that clean magazines charge a great deal more for their advertising space than vulgar magazines, because the people who read salacious trash are not, as a rule, prosperous enough to be in the market for anything expensive, you may be inclined to pump him for some more information related thereunto. He has it, and will tell you if you ask him. Encourage the librarian to tell you what sort of books are being read, and by whom. Go down into the railroad-yards, and spend an hour in the cab of a switch-engine, some night. Probe for an invitation to attend a meeting of the Bricklayers' Union, and sit around with them, for an hour's chat, after the session. If you are looking for live illustrative matter to put into your sermons, go out and get it where it is! That is precisely what our Master did, and apparently His dignity did not suffer thereby. You will find more sermon material on the streets than you can ever dig out of books. It is unnecessary that you should have all your experience of life at second-hand.

Now, as to process. Perhaps you feel that you are not quite up to sermon composition on Monday. That is a matter of temperament. If you think you should keep Monday free of all thought about sermons, follow your inclination. Tuesday morning, however, you should begin to draw rough "blue-prints" of the thing, so that you can be thinking about it, in orderly fashion, while you go about your other tasks. Collect your materials early. Attend to all the necessary research as soon as possible. By Thursday you may find that what you thought was the mere episodal incident in your sermon has become the pièce de résistance. If so, you should discover that fact on Thursday, and not on Saturday night, about nine-thirty. On Thursday, you should be writing. Write it all —all!—with all the i's dotted, and all the t's crossed! Whatever policy you may pursue, later on, be sure to write it out in full during the early years of your ministry. If you wish to be unencumbered with notes or a manuscript, in the pulpit, that is all very well; but write! This gives you a chance to enlarge and enrich your vocabulary, and to acquire precision and clearness of statement. It will help insure you against that chief menace of extempore preaching—repetition.

Do not be afraid of the drudgery of writing with a pencil, sometimes. Machines can be driven very rapidly, with a little practice. Many a minister, skilled in the facile use of all ten fingers on the keyboard of his machine, preaches an extempore sermon, on Sunday, even though he may read his manuscript with the most slavish attention to its lines. Composition with a pencil is good discipline. It improves one's style, mostly because it makes one think more slowly.

Be aware that the introduction to your sermon is going to be a guarantee of its success or failure. If you secure the attention of your audience in the first three sentences, you stand a good chance of keeping it. Your own experience will certify that it is at the very beginning of the sermon—before the preacher has yet had time to make his case—that the auditor goes wool-gathering. The same rule applies here that governs your interest in a magazine article. If your interest is stirred by the first sentence, you are likely to read on.

There is quite a different reaction produced whether your first sentence, on Sunday morning, is, "Moses had now been wandering about in the Mountains of Midian for forty years," or "Last Thursday afternoon, about five o'clock, two men met down here at the corner of High and Main, and one asked the other what he thought about the justice of the income tax." Both of these leads may be introductions to the same sermon bearing upon the responsibility of men to put back, into their civilization, something commensurate to that which they have taken out. But one lead will prove to be an anæsthetic, while the other is a stimulant. Don't begin your sermon with platitudes, maxims, adages, abstractions, or any other old stuff that makes the people yawn.

You will have frequent occasion to narrate Bible stories. All history—that in the Bible not excepted—is biography. Make these ancient people live! If you cannot present Nehemiah in such a manner that the people will see him as a real, flesh-and-blood, one-hundred-and-seventy-five-pound man, it will not be for lack of data concerning him. These ancients must not be portrayed as a group of marble statues, or enhaloed unrealities. They were real people. Make them breathe, and talk, and act!

Beware of too much poetry! The last refuge of a lazy preacher, on Saturday night, when he knows that his sermon has not yet been provided with a convincing terminal, is to haul out his "World's Best Poetry," and begin to thumb it through in search of a jingle wherewith to finish his discourse. The more gifted he is in the art of reading poetry, the more he will be menaced by this temptation. Presently the people become accustomed to the idea that when he arrives at the poem, he is through, and they can go home to dinner. Listen: that last sentence must always be a surprise! You are to be the only man in the church who knows that it is the last one! Be careful about falling into habits which inform the congregation exactly when you are tapering off, and making ready to stop. If you do not watch yourself, you will always quit in the same way. The congregation will have come to understand that when you shift your voice to a slightly lower register, and achieve a certain degree of fervency in your utterance, it is high time they began to fumble about, under the seats, feeling for their over-shoes. Surprise them with the novelty of the sermon's close, just as you surprise them with the originality of its introduction.

You cannot afford to use canned illustrations. If you haven't enough imagination to capital-ize your own experiences and observations of life, it is exceedingly doubtful if you could tell anybody else's story in a convincing manner. Now and again, in your reading, you will come across a yarn that does good business with your own emotions. It is entirely permissible to use it. Remember where you found it; and, when it fits exactly into what you happen to be doing, tell it as effectively as you know how. But to take down a volume of "sermonic illus-trations," in cold blood, after you had come to a standstill in your homiletic production and the thing seems to have hung on a dead centre, and go on a still hunt for some story that might presumably be twisted into some slight sem-blance of aptitude to your thesis—this sort of procedure would be merely ridiculous if it were not so dreadfully immoral!

After a preacher has been in the business for five years, he is likely to observe that he has only two or three pet themes. No matter what hole he goes in at, he is sure to come out, at length, from his favorite exit. The congregation learns, after a while, that no vigorous intellectual exercise will be required of it. The auditor needs do nothing but trudge, mentally, to the place where he knows the preacher is going to arrive, and there await his coming. One man is pretty certain, no matter what motion is before the house, to instruct the secretary to cast the ballot of the assembly for Brotherhood of Man. Of the half-dozen poems he knows, by heart, the one he recites most often is: "The house by the side of the road." This is very good gospel; but this is not the whole gospel, by any means. Another man seems committed to the belief that his mission is largely one of consolation. He is always praying for the sorrowing, and addressing himself to the depressed. His slogan is: "Let not your heart be troubled." This, too, is good gospel; but not all of it. Still another thinks it is his manifest destiny to encourage the more ardent and effective practice of prayer. Whatever he is doing, in the pulpit, he can be depended upon to manœuvre himself about, from one vantage to another, until he arrives at the prayer concept where he feels perfectly at home, and at his best.

Can you not be more versatile than that? The gospel you preach is inexhaustible. It touches all life, from hub to rim. Your congregation is composed of all sorts of people.

Some of them can be challenged, some inspired, some led; some must be driven. Do not commit John Brand's blunder in trying to make everybody in your constituency decide on "all or nothing!" You can make apostles out of some of them; others may be teachers; but "are all apostles?"—"are all teachers?" Sometimes you should preach repentance. Be careful that you distinguish between repentance and remorse. Ordinarily, the "propulsive power of a new ideal" will take people further toward spirituality than any introspection urged upon them whereby they are required to examine their sins with tweezers and microscope. Vary the diet. Do not permit yourself to be carried away with the infatuation of some special line of research.

Fresh from the seminary, you are full of theology. You should be. That is what theological seminaries are for. This is the foundation—the flooring of your whole homiletic life; but you must not tear this up and hurl it at the people, Sunday after Sunday. Keep it in mind that many of the terms which have been in common use, in the school of the prophets, are utterly incomprehensible to the average layman. Keep close to the vernacular. If the people seem dull, and you are disposed to wonder if you are not casting your pearls before swine, examine your pearls first before passing judgment.

Whether the people will listen to you with confidence and respect, or with an attitude of distrust and irritation, is going to depend upon the manner of your speech, tone, gesture, and general appraisal of life.   You can declare your beliefs with a growl, and lay down your principles with a bang, and excite resentment.   If you are obviously tolerant of others' views, apparently eager to learn, and not too cock-sure of everything you say, you may take almost any position, within reason, and retain the friendliness and regard of your congregation.

Doubtless you are ambitious to become a great preacher.   This hope does you credit. Keep it in mind that men may be very useful without becoming conspicuous outside the bounds of their own parishes.   Ambition is attended by some grave dangers.   Keep your ambition preserved in a solution of humility. Remember that the most eminent preacher who ever lived humbled Himself and became of no reputation.   If it comes to pass that by industry, application, and the proper use of your talents, you should become a ranking member of our profession, known, far and wide, as a pulpit genius, so be it.   If that never comes to pass, and you spend your ministry merely going about doing good, your name unknown except to those whose hearts you have touched by personal contact, you may find satisfaction in remembering that "many there be who have no memorial; who perished as though they had never been; but their righteousness hath not been forgotten, and the honor of their deeds cannot be blotted out."